IMS: Implementing and Operating Using PAS 99

Integrated Management Systems Series

The Integrated Management Systems (IMS) series of books provides practical guidance and advice on integrating the systems operating within an organization. The IMS series provides a framework into which additional management systems can be incorporated.

Each volume is written by an acknowledged expert in the field. The series editor is David Smith of iMS Risk Solutions Ltd, who has been involved in writing management system standards since the early 1990s and is himself the author of a number of BSI books on the subject.

IMS: A Framework for Integrated Management Systems
IMS: Implementing and Operating Using PAS 99
IMS: The Excellence Model
IMS: Creating a Manual
IMS: Customer Satisfaction
IMS: Continual Improvement through Auditing
IMS: Risk Management for Good Governance
IMS: Information Security
IMS: Managing Food Safety

Integrated Management Systems Series

IMS: Implementing and Operating Using PAS 99

David Smith and Rob Politowski

iMS Risk Solutions Ltd

BSi Business Information

First published as *IMS: Implementing and Operating* in the UK in 2002
Second edition first published in 2007

by
BSI
389 Chiswick High Road
London W4 4AL

Typeset in Gill Sans and Century Schoolbook by Monolith
Printed in Great Britain by MPG Books, Bodmin, Cornwall

British Library Cataloguing in Publication Data
A catalogue record for this book is available from the British Library

ISBN 978-0-580-50949-0

Acknowledgements

The authors wish to acknowledge the sterling support provided by Chris Millidge in the production of this book. His insightful comments and editing have been a consistent source of help and inspiration. Christine Cox and her colleagues at BSI have provided the continual encouragement necessary to complete the project.

Contents

1. Introduction

Organizations use management system standards for a variety of reasons: they may have decided that these are the best way to manage a particular discipline, or it may be in order to demonstrate their commitment to issues such as quality (ISO 9001:2000), information security (ISO 27001) or whatever standard they perceive to be of advantage to the business. Those with multiple systems have typically found it difficult to integrate the common requirements and incorporate them into the overall management system. This book gives some simple guidance on how this may be achieved, using as an example three of the more commonly used specifications – quality, environment, and occupational health and safety (OH&S). PAS 99 (see below) extends the application to additional areas such as food safety and service management. The methodology is equally applicable to other specifications and also to those functions that are not the subject of a formal management systems standard.

The aim of every top manager must surely be to have the organization working together as a single team with clearly understood objectives. This is often easier to achieve in a small organization, but growth tends to bring the separation of functions where unity of action and purpose is more difficult to achieve in large organizations. Different management systems each tend to have their own manager and supporting organization, and this is true of such functions as finance and marketing as well as quality, environment or OH&S.

The subject of integrated management systems is in some respects controversial and can evoke strong reactions in respect of the terminology, the approach and the models used. It can also provoke rivalry between those who have traditionally managed individual elements and see their role and system being displaced.

The principles behind the integration of management systems as defined in the various ISO management system standards are given in the first book in this series, *IMS: A Framework for Integrated Management Systems – Background to PAS 99 and its application*. The present book concentrates on how to approach integrating systems based on the standards dealing with quality, environment, and OH&S, so that they can form part of a unified management system for the organization as a whole.

Since the first edition of this book was produced, a publicly available specification (PAS) entitled *PAS 99: Specification of common management system requirements as a framework for integration* was published by the British Standards Institution (BSI) in the summer of 2006. PAS 99 builds upon the framework found in ISO Guide 72 and that in the first edition of this book. PAS 99 sets out to formalize more precisely the common requirements for those operating multiple systems such as ISO 9001, ISO 14001, BS OHSAS 18001:2007, BS ISO/IEC 20000-1:2005, BS EN ISO 22000:2005 and ISO 27001.

The framework offered in PAS 99 is one that can be used to integrate not only those management systems to which you already subscribe but also those that you may wish to adopt in the future. The methodology offered here should help with the process of integrating the requirements into your business management, integrated management system (IMS) or any management system specification you wish to adopt. In the longer term, the issue of compatibility will be addressed more and more by the standards-writing organizations, which have recognized this as an important issue. There are other books in this series that deal with systems relating to other subjects such as food safety, risk management and information security.

This unified system can also incorporate those management disciplines where there are as yet no formal management system standards, such as sales and marketing or accounts or personnel.

Every organization will start from a different point: some will have virtually nothing in place in the way of formalized management systems; others will have well-developed systems encompassing two or more disciplines. This book is written so that readers can pick and choose what they need to help them achieve their objectives.

An IMS is designed to improve the performance of the organization: it must be effective and efficient and should deliver better results to all stakeholders. If it does not do this it has failed in its purpose.

The business case

There has to be a business case for implementing any form of management system and a formal IMS is no different in this respect.

Before implementing any system an organization will have considered its specific needs. If the organization is essentially a one-person business, formal written procedures are obviously not essential for all the processes. The larger and more complex the organization the greater will be the need for systems in its management. The business case for implementing a specific system may have been based on a variety of reasons: financial savings, efficiency, productivity, effectiveness or even customer or legal requirements.

The case for implementing an integrated system as distinct from standalone management systems will be based primarily on the internal benefits to the organization. There is not likely to be any significant pressure from customers or external agencies to integrate. The decision will be based on the expected benefits that will arise at a number of different levels.

PAS 99 states that it

> has been produced to help organizations to achieve benefits from consolidating the common requirements in all management system standards/specifications and managing these requirements effectively. The benefits may include:
>
> a) improved business focus;
> b) a more holistic approach to managing business risks;
> c) less conflict between systems;
> d) reduced duplication and bureaucracy;
> e) more effective and efficient audits both internally and externally.

In practice the benefits are likely to be seen in the following areas:

Tangible costs. Avoidance of duplication in systems, for example audit, document control.
Operational benefits. Helps to ensure that all the consequences of any action are taken into account, for example a design change in the product may not only affect quality but also environment and OH&S, or a process

change where the environmental effects are obvious may also affect OH&S.
Management benefits. Separate 'empires' for quality, OH&S, etc. are avoided – all are seen as part of the overall management system of the organization. The involvement of employees in the various stages of the process can develop a team attitude in the staff and positive identification with the aims of the organization.
Strategic benefits. The adoption of future management system standards will be easier, and therefore cheaper, so an organization will be encouraged to adopt any standard that would be beneficial; all systems are seen as part of a single management system contributing to the continual improvement in the results of the organization.

Some stakeholders (including insurers) may increasingly welcome the reassurance that an integrated system provides.

The unity of purpose of all employees is emphasized rather than their functional duties, contributing to a *holistic* team approach.

In many respects organizations adopting this approach are introducing a risk management system for the business. This is being increasingly demanded and has been a requirement for health and safety for many years. The benefits of effective risk management have been increasingly recognized by capital markets, regulators and investors around the world and are often a requirement for stock exchange listing. The risk assessment approach is progressively being used in all activities of an organization and can be invaluable in reducing the likelihood of claims as well as direct and indirect costs arising from such issues as failures, business interruption, accident/incident losses or environmental disasters. It is also an important feature in maintaining the reputation of the organization. Both the International Organization for Standardization (ISO) and BSI are in the process of producing guidance standards on risk management (BS 31100) that embrace the controls needed to manage operational risks as well as those of a strategic nature.

Organizations typically consider their top three risks to be:

1. reputation (loss of);
2. people (sabotage, incompetence, loss of crucial resource); and
3. compliance issues.

Reputation is not a subject you can control in its own right and loss of reputation is likely to arise through failure to manage a specific risk or risks. A holistic approach to managing risks can reduce the likelihood of reputational damage and an IMS approach offers many benefits as outlined above.

Why an integrated management system?

The background to the concept of IMS standards is described at some length in the first book in this series, *IMS: Principles of Integrated Management Systems – Background to PAS 99 and its application*, so only a summary will be included here.

For most organizations their first encounter with a formal management system standard was with the quality standard ISO 9000 series or its predecessors. Many thousands of organizations adopted these standards – initially almost exclusively in manufacturing, but increasingly in services, local government, education and the professions. There are now some 700,000 organizations registered to these standards around the world.

The next management system standard to appear concerned environmental management. This went through a number of versions finally ending up as the ISO 14000 series. Many of those who sought to implement this standard had already adopted ISO 9001, and the similarities between the two led to consideration of the advantages that could arise if they could be managed together rather than through separate departments within a company. A lot of administrative duplication and the management diversion caused by multiple assessments and surveillances could be avoided.

In practice, however, it was found although there were indeed many similarities between the two standards there were also significant differences, which made a unified system difficult to achieve. Differences in structure and even terminology created problems. Clearly these could only get worse as more management system standards appeared, such as those concerned with health and safety, human resources, information security and so on. Some aspects of this problem have been addressed and recognized in the later versions of the standards (compare ISO 9001:2000 with the 1994 version, or ISO 14001:2004 with that of 1996).

Following industry surveys in the UK, a report was published (MacGregor Associates, 1997) that concluded that total integration in the sense of having a single overall standard covering quality, environment, etc. was not a practical proposition. Instead, management system standards should in future work towards alignment. Definitions and vocabulary should be consistent and a common structure followed. This meant that the common elements could, if required, be managed as an entity with the specific requirements being clear for each discipline.

These recommendations have since become generally accepted and the ISO Technical Management Board published ISO Guide 72. One of the aims of this publication was to assist those involved in writing management system standards to ensure compatibility and assist in ease of use. This compatibility will clearly be progressive and it can now be hoped that management system standards will be easier to incorporate into a single IMS. The next revisions of ISO 9001 (due in 2008) and ISO 14001 (due in 2012) are intended to produce standards with even greater alignment.

The use of common terms and definitions and the potential for using a common numbering system for clauses within standards could lead to systems being standardized, but even in the current versions of these standards a significant proportion is common, although of course the specific elements of the discipline need to be addressed separately. The combined state is shown on the right-hand side of Figure 1.1. How large the common element of your overall system is depends to some extent on the needs of the organization.

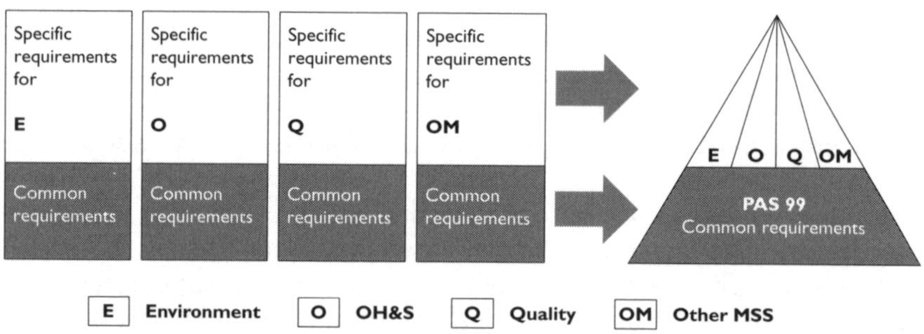

Source: PAS 99, Figure 1

Figure 1.1 – Illustration of how the common requirements of multiple management system standards/specifications (MSS) can be integrated into one common system

Many organizations want just one management system that is both efficient and effective in delivering the objectives set to meet the various stakeholder needs. The framework provided in PAS 99 should enable this aim to be realized.

The approach

Even if your organization is already certificated to, say, ISO 9001 and ISO 14001, it is recommended that the implementation of an integrated system is carried out by focusing on one discipline at a time. The important thing is to recognize that there is to be an IMS, and that each discipline is to form part of that integrated system. To start by amalgamating two disciplines without reference to an overall integrated system may well not be the best way forward.

It is clear that if the project is to be successful the head of the organization must be seen to be heavily involved. He or she may appoint a project manager to see the whole process through, and the existing quality manager, safety manager, etc. will clearly be much involved. However, the object of the exercise is to improve the performance of the business, which is the direct responsibility of the chief executive and the top management team. The purely administrative work may be delegated, but the commitment from the top must always be in evidence.

One point has to be made clear at the outset: there is no right or wrong approach. The objective is to produce an IMS that is right for your organization. The aim of this book is to help you to arrive at that system, which will then be right for you and your organization even though it may be completely unsuitable for someone else. The scope you adopt can be far greater than those areas currently covered by formal management systems.

A research study undertaken by Karapetrovic et al. (2006) gives some indication of the approaches adopted by organizations in the absence of any guidance. This is not to imply that any guidance should insist on any one approach. It is interesting to note that contrary to some learned views expressed on quality and environmental standards, the 'process' approach of ISO 9001 and the plan-do-check-act (PDCA) risk-based or system approach of ISO 14001 are compatible and can be used very effectively together.

The methodology adopted in this book acknowledges the move towards the process approach now evident in ISO 9001:2000 and ISO 9004:2000. It equally recognizes that the PDCA approach has many merits, particularly where risk needs to be taken into account. These two approaches complement each other in an integrated system.

The process approach is useful in identifying the issues you need to manage, and the model can be extended to encompass all interested parties, not just customers. Figure 1.2 is a variation on that shown in ISO 9001:2000 including a broader scope. In contrast to the above-mentioned standards, it recognizes the need to implement control measures appropriate to satisfying the organizational needs as well as those of the interested parties. This is always a compromise and an element of risk is inevitably involved. A framework for managing these risks, i.e. those aspects that could have a significant impact, is given below and in more detail in PAS 99, Clause 4.

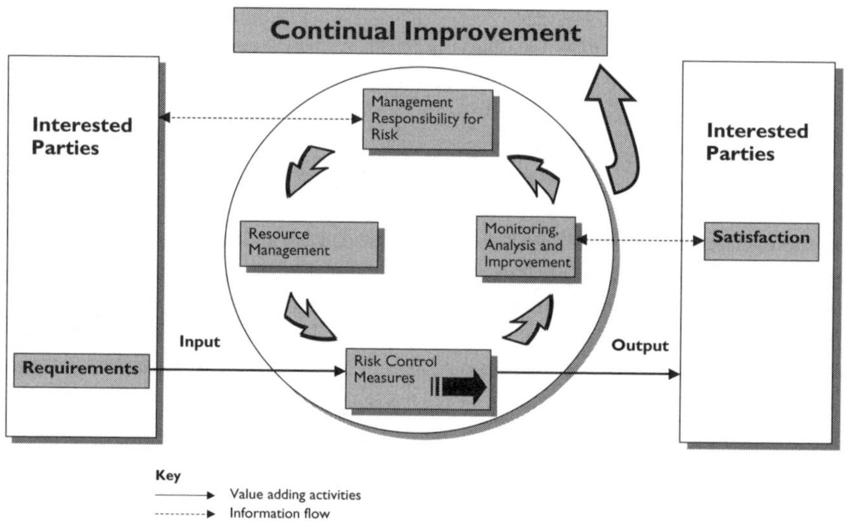

Figure 1.2 – Model of a process-based quality management system

For many organizations there will be benefits in looking at their aspects collectively. By aspect we mean those issues that have the potential to cause harm to the product, damage to the environment or otherwise affect the desired output.

The process approach for identifying the aspects and establishing impacts (risks) and necessary control measures is illustrated in Figure 1.4.

The individual boxes will be the signposts to the implementation programme given in the book. However, it is first necessary to understand the process approach. A simple model is the making of a cup of tea, as shown in Figure 1.3.

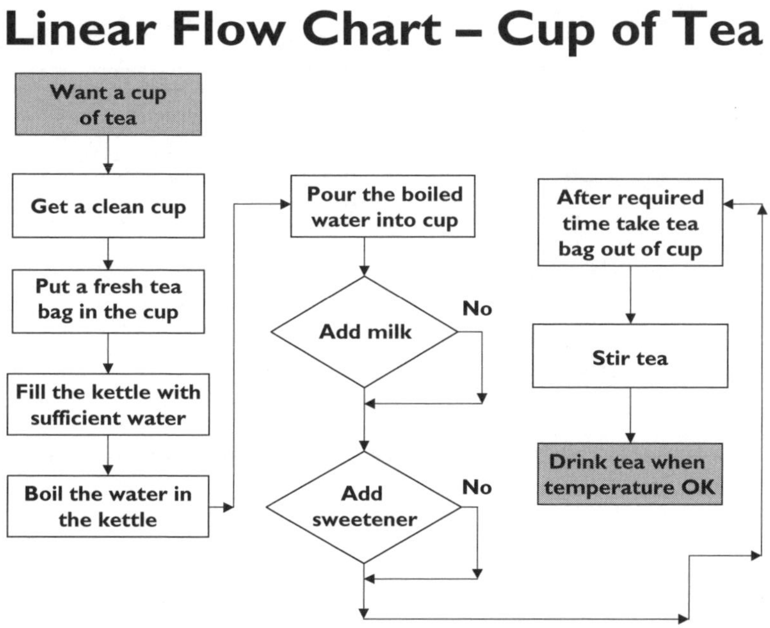

Figure 1.3 – Simple example of a flow chart

Obviously there are a number of variations on the process but, accepting this model as being correct, we can see it is possible to cover all activities in such a manner. These include transport, storage, office, paperwork, etc. Each of the stages between start and finish could affect the quality and many have aspects that also relate to environmental and OH&S issues.

Using this methodology, the implementation of an IMS is shown in Figure 1.4. In reality this will involve a number of sub-processes that are not shown for the sake of simplicity. The chart could be particularly useful for those who have little in place by way of a management system.

Figure 1.4 – Steps towards implementation of an IMS

The PAS 99 model

PAS 99 gives a model for encompassing the common elements of an IMS in a PDCA approach. It is not the only approach but is a simple framework that enables the process approach of ISO 9001:2000, and the system approach of ISO 14001 and BS OHSAS 18001 to be encompassed. It can also just as conveniently accommodate the organization's other management disciplines.

The main headings for each element of the framework are shown in Figure 1.5. In subsequent chapters, the details of each element are shown and discussed in turn.

PAS 99 offers a guide to what the common elements of your IMS should include and what other requirements should be addressed. Each specific discipline may well need additional procedures, documentation, etc. depending on the specific requirements of the formal standard embraced within the system. Where appropriate later chapters in this book end with

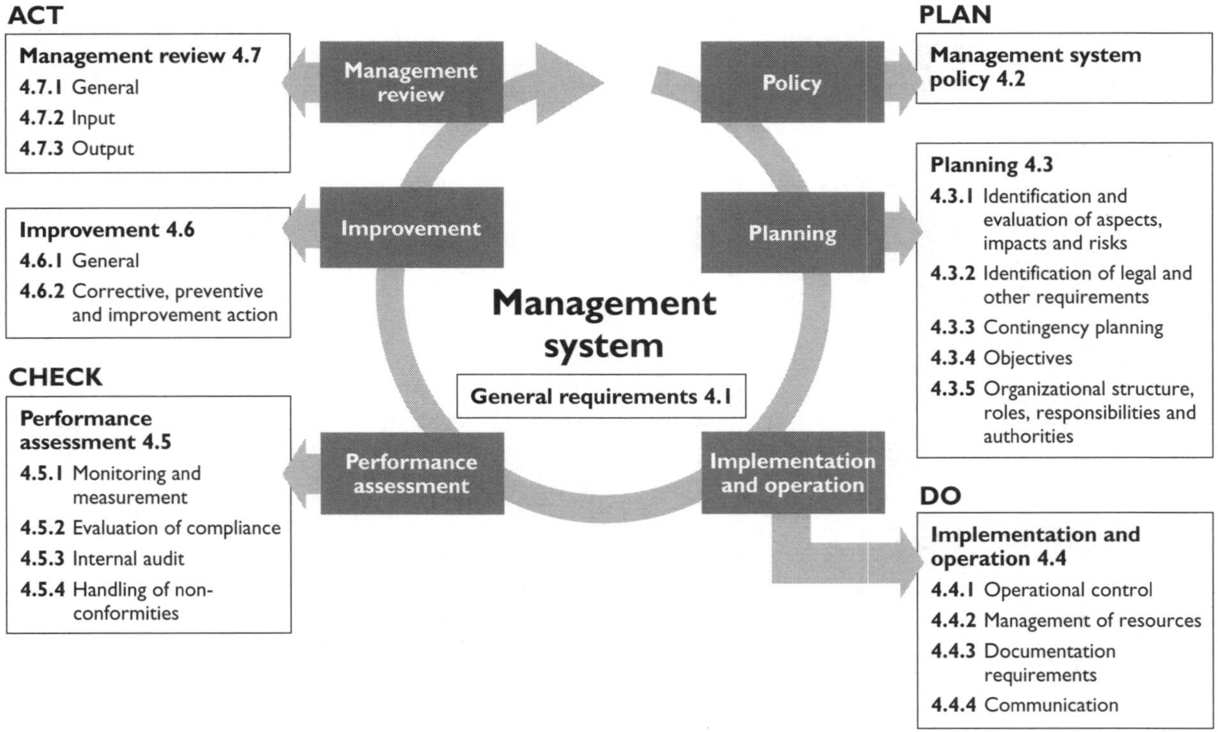

Source: PAS 99, Figure 2

Figure 1.5 – Illustration of how PDCA and the common requirements combine to give the outline structure of the management system

a list of additional requirements for ISO 9001:2000, ISO 14001:2004 and BS OHSAS 18001:2007.

This guide is in no way prescriptive, either in content or in the order in which activities are included. Some organizations may find it totally suitable for their purpose, whilst others may find it too complex or otherwise not appropriate. It should, however, be useful as a checklist and guide to make sure that nothing important has been missed.

The basis of the management system should be as described in Section 4.1 of PAS 99.

There is a need to decide the scope that your IMS will cover remembering that it is not acceptable to restrict the scope of environmental, and OH&S systems such as by subcontracting risks to the other parties. To some extent the scope will become obvious as you carry out your initial status review (ISR) and gap analysis (see Chapter 2).

In the PAS 99 framework the element 'Management System' identifies the system in broad terms. It requires that the organization puts in a management system that includes the identification of the processes needed and the sequence interaction, etc. as shown in Figure 1.5.

2. Getting started

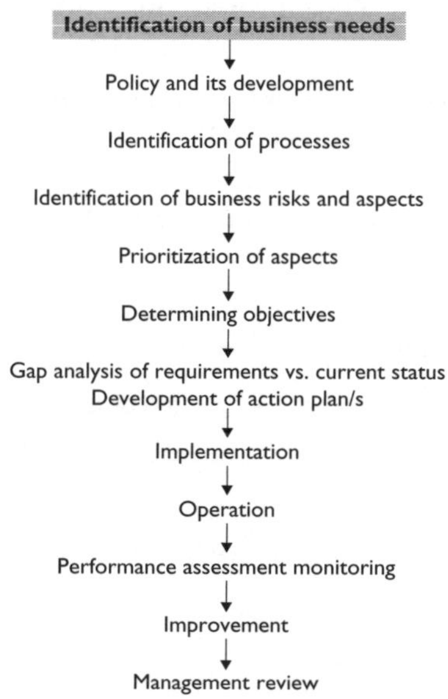

Figure 2.1

(Figure 2.1 follows the logic of Figure 1.6 but shows the initial stages in more detail.)

This is a chicken and egg situation. Although each standard shows a particular way forward, in reality you will need to approach it in the light of the nature and background of your particular organization. Those with established systems will have a framework for addressing the requirements of one or more management system standards. For beginners the current arrangements for delivery to customers' specifications, or for OH&S, should be useful.

The ISR is the recommended starting point. In all management systems the management review, which both ends the process and starts the next cycle (see Figure 1.5), is a strong element and the same applies here.

For those coming from a quality background, the process is similar but the use of the ISR is to establish where the organization is now and where it wants to be. In simple terms the ISR should:

- determine what is needed for the IMS (i.e. what do we want);
- determine what the organization has in place at the current time (i.e. what have we in place already that can be used in the IMS).

This is a simple gap analysis, which can be expanded as the system develops to include best practice and the effectiveness and efficiency of the current arrangements.

This is the first step of the project plan for implementing an IMS, and we need a route map from where we are to where we want to be.

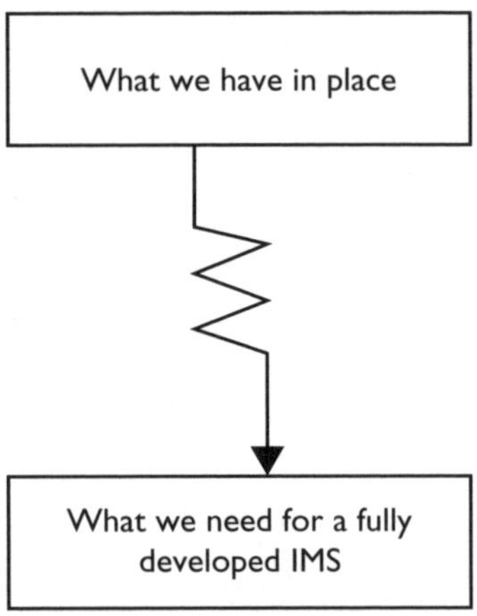

Figure 2.2

The business needs should not be underestimated here. There is certainly a need to control quality, reduce impact on the environment and minimize OH&S risk. However, if you have the best-quality product in the world, with absolute control over the environmental and OH&S aspects, it may be that no one will buy your product or service because it is too expensive. There has to be a balance. All organizations and individuals have to take risks. Travelling by car is a far greater risk than most other risks faced during employment. Switching a light on means you impact on the environment; not switching it on can mean not being able to work, or gives rise to OH&S issues.

It is a matter of judgement for the organization and the interested parties to determine what it should strive for and what is acceptable. The business needs will normally need to take account of the concerns of, for example:

- customers;
- suppliers/contractors;
- neighbours;
- banks;
- insurers;
- regulators;
- shareholders (including society if it is a government body);
- society;
- the workforce;
- statutory business watchdogs.

The stages in between the positions shown in Figure 2.1 in the plan very much depend on what you have to contribute to the final IMS system, i.e. how big the gap is between the boxes shown in Figure 2.2.

3. General requirements

Identification of business needs
↓
Policy and its development
↓
Identification of processes
↓
Identification of business risks and aspects
↓
Prioritization of aspects
↓
Determining objectives
↓
Gap analysis of requirements vs. current status
Development of action plan/s
↓
Implementation
↓
Operation
↓
Performance assessment monitoring
↓
Improvement
↓
Management review

Figure 3.1

The planning stage is in many respects most important and demanding when first starting to implement any management system. When embarking upon the implementation of an integrated system, careful planning is obviously vital. Once a clear view has been obtained of what it is intended to achieve and the means of achievement, the implementation of the plan can be undertaken with confidence. There is a need to gain commitment to the plan and to take on board any reasonable concerns expressed by those who have a specific interest in one discipline. They will need reassurance that the new system has the tangible benefits that have been described in Chapter 1.

You need to identify clearly not only what the IMS needs to support but also what is to be done, by whom, how and when, and what resources are needed. The subject is accordingly considered in some detail.

Although there are written requirements in various standards, these will not ensure success even when they are fully met. Examples abound of organizations with very elaborate and exhaustive systems that fail because no one is committed to them. This book does not attempt to provide a comprehensive method of gaining commitment and a positive culture.

Top management need to demonstrate commitment in practice, encouraging positive actions as well as dealing with failure. Apart from demonstrating commitment by walking around, inspecting and observing, they should participate or encourage other senior managers and operators to take an active part in identifying and prioritizing aspects. In those areas of highest risk and involving the most important aspects, top management should take an active and prominent role, even if specific tasks are delegated.

Some positive steps to ensure total involvement and commitment include:

- encouraging an open, 'no-blame' culture;
- leading by example;
- giving constructive feedback;
- setting out clear policies;
- recognizing the strengths (and weaknesses) of the existing organizational culture;
- encouraging team work and team loyalty;
- recognizing good work;
- introducing a consistent and fair approach;
- involving people at all levels in the organization;
- developing a cross-functional approach to problem identification and embedding new practices;
- thinking laterally.

Another essential element in the implementation will be the training of employees, and this needs to be taken into account at the planning stage. One of the benefits you are looking for in an integrated system is the positive culture and team attitude from every employee. If they are to be expected to contribute to activities such as identifying risks or safety aspects, for example, they will probably need some initial training in what is expected of them. They must also be convinced of the purpose of the whole exercise, and you may need to remove any suspicions that it is aimed at staff reduction rather than helping all parties to achieve their objectives.

As new parts of the system are implemented, further training will probably be necessary to ensure that employees are able to operate it with confidence. It is a common experience, unfortunately, for a new system to be devised and implemented and then fail completely because of inadequate training of the people who are to operate it. This has been particularly common with new computer systems where there have been cost overruns in the initial stages and the employer has attempted to recoup some of the costs by 'saving' on the training programme, resulting in total system failure. To economize on training can prove a very expensive saving.

Planning the project

There is much merit in adopting a formal project management approach using techniques such as those described in BS 6079 *Part 1 – Guide to Project Management*.

If, for example, it was decided to implement an OH&S management system as a start within a generic framework, the initial plan could look like Figure 3.2.

A key person needs to be in charge of the implementation and set a realistic schedule for the system to be operational. This person may be a senior line manager or the quality, safety or environmental manager, provided they have the necessary skills and vision to think more broadly than their specific management discipline. Ideally, the person chosen for the implementation programme should have experience of project management.

If you are starting from scratch, trying to take everything on at once may be far too ambitious – unless the organization is relatively small and uncomplicated. How you move forward will depend on many issues. You may find yourself in one of these three situations:

No system at all and few controls in place. In this case you will need to go through the whole process as described in this book, starting with a consideration of the needs of your business and then how you are going to meet those needs through the introduction of management systems.

One-discipline management system. This is possibly the easiest scenario. Here the process is one of aligning the current system with the framework. The new system should be operated to ensure it is working efficiently and effectively. Then it is the planning stage, particularly aspect identification and prioritization that needs to be revisited, taking in the aspects of the other disciplines that need to be incorporated.

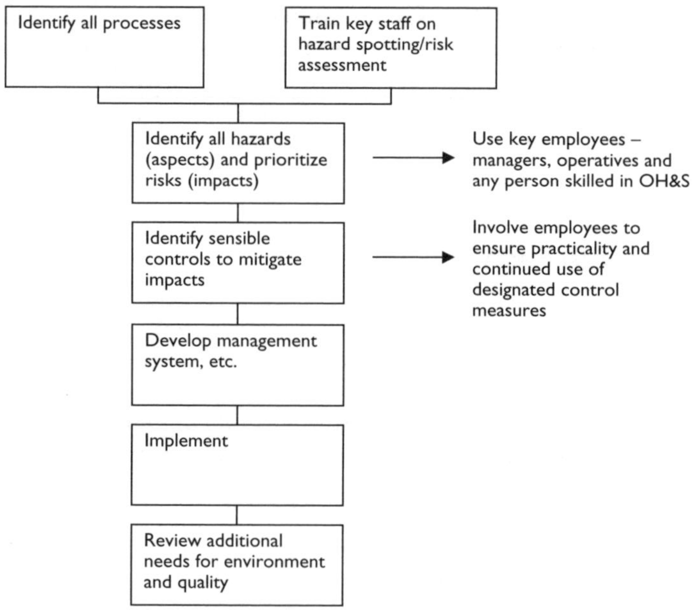

Figure 3.2

Multi-discipline system. Although in this situation you will have all the management system controls you need, the politics and the culture need to be considered extremely carefully when embarking on the project. This cannot be overstated. The people who have built the existing systems may quite genuinely believe theirs is superb and that everything should be based on their approach. Particular difficulties can arise from those with effective quality systems trying to expand to cover other disciplines. Often the quality management system (QMS) has a restricted scope covering a particular product or service while an environmental management system (EMS) and an occupational health and safety management system (OH&SMS) require much broader scopes and, by their very nature, cannot be so confined.

If excellent systems exist with a positive culture throughout the organization then it is essential that you move forward with great care and consideration to all parties. Moreover, if the current system(s) is certificated you need to make sure any transition does not compromise the registration.

It is manifestly important to implement changes and the transition as a carefully planned project. Again, we recommend that you establish your framework on the basis of one of the systems, ensuring the wording is consistent with the other disciplines to be covered.

Identification of processes

Figure 3.3 expands upon the identification of the process shown in Figure 3.1.

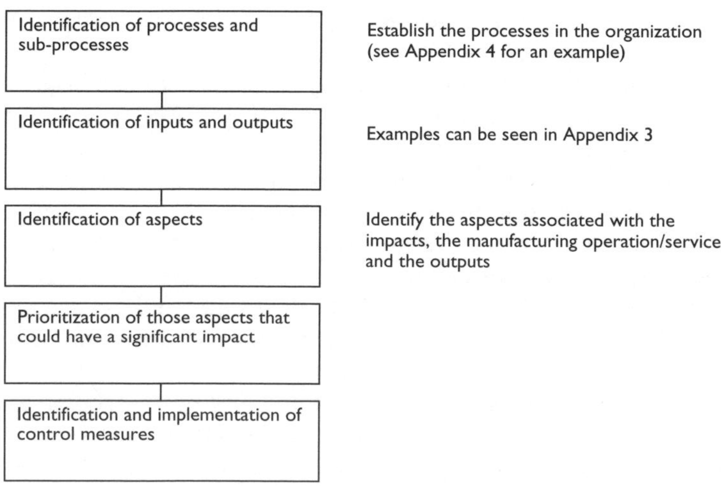

Figure 3.3

The first stage is process mapping. It may be that you are most aware in the first instance of the goods and services you buy in (inputs) and the goods and services you provide to your customers (outputs). You will also be aware of the processes undertaken within the organization but perhaps not in the detail necessary to establish the individual aspects that need to be evaluated (see Figure 3.4).

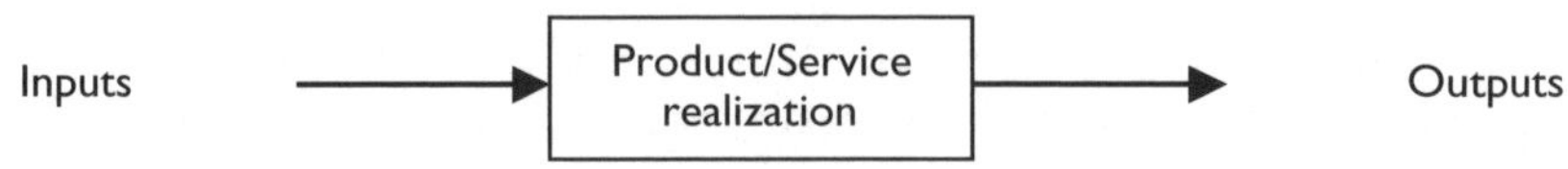

Figure 3.4

The realization of the product/service may be simple, but is more likely to be complex with many elements each involving their own inputs and outputs. To avoid overload at this stage only the significant elements should be considered.

Figure 3.5 is an elaboration of the ISO 9001/ISO 9004 model of process management, showing how the organization needs to manage its processes to satisfy the requirements and expectations of the various interested parties, and to achieve continual improvement.

For those from a quality background the main thrust has of necessity been to control the processes carried out within the organization. We can consider the aspects of these processes as *direct aspects*.

Those processes that are not within direct control of the organization can be equally important and affect its fortunes. For instance a good product or service that is misused by the customer can reflect on the organization and give it and its product or service a bad name. So in some cases aspects that are not directly under the control of the organization need to be evaluated and the organization may reasonably be expected to influence its suppliers, contractors, users and customers. These aspects can be considered as *indirect aspects*. Both direct and indirect aspects need to be taken into account and the scope will vary as that for environment will differ from that of quality, for example.

Think of the organization as a unit as shown in Figure 3.5, and draw up a process diagram such as shown in Figure 3.6. Do not forget to include such issues as storage of fuel, goods, waste, etc. and maintenance activities. Figure 3.5 relates mainly to environmental features, but similar diagrams can be prepared in relation to each of the other disciplines involved.

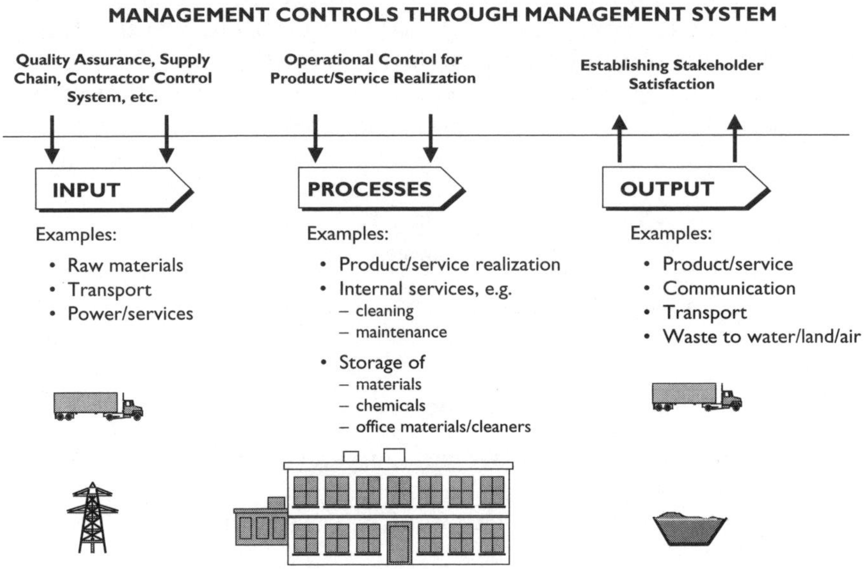

Figure 3.5

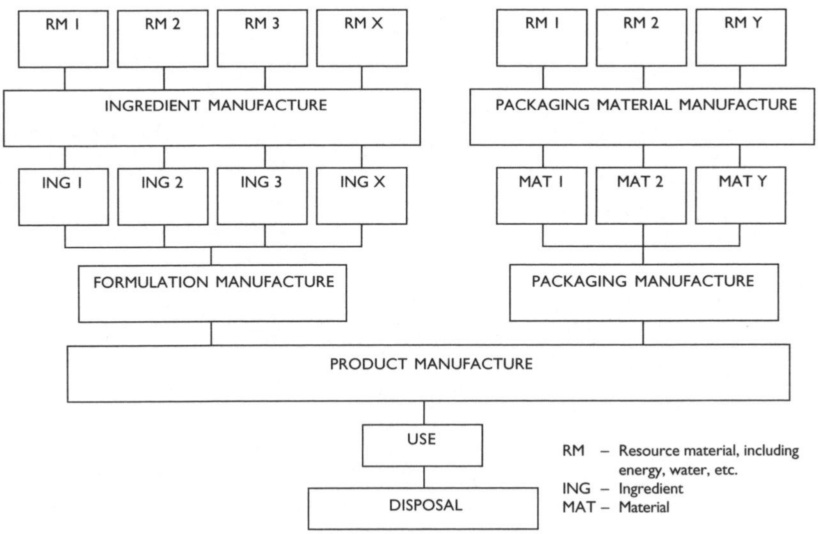

Figure 3.6

A picture such as Figure 3.7 should finally emerge for the main operations of the organization. While this illustration refers to manufacturing, exactly the same principles apply in the provision of services or any other non-manufacturing situation. This should be developed so that you can consider all the individual processes in more detail.

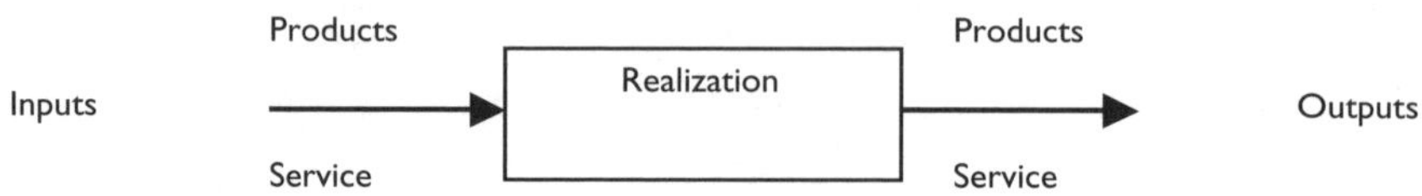

Figure 3.7

It may help if you list the inputs, operations and outputs in a table format to ensure that nothing has been missed.

An example of the identification of processes in a manufacturing business is given in Appendix 3.

4. Management system policy

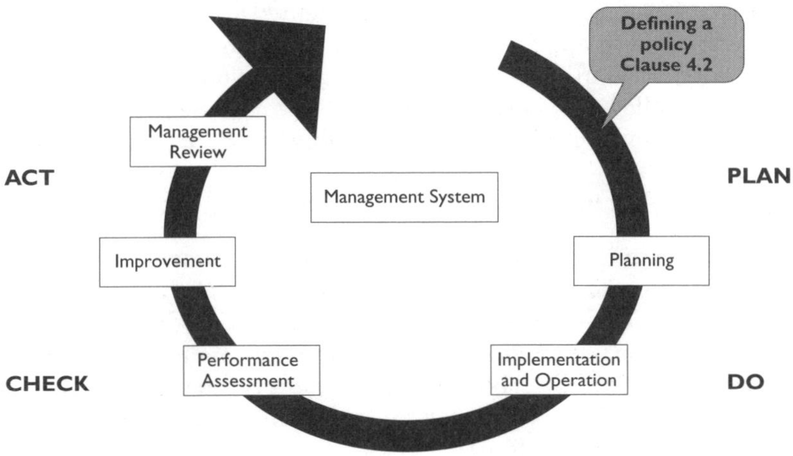

Figure 4.1

Top management shall define the policy of the organization in respect of its management system and ensure that it:

a) is appropriate to the organization's activities, products and services;
b) includes a commitment to comply with all relevant legal and other requirements to which the organization subscribes and to continually improve the effectiveness of the management system;

c) provides a framework for establishing and reviewing objectives;
d) is communicated to all persons working for or on behalf of the organization;
e) is regularly reviewed for continuing suitability. (4.2)

An organization's existing policy in any discipline will reflect its maturity, its size and the nature of the risks. There is no requirement to have a single integrated policy, but many organizations choose to take this route. Care therefore needs to be taken in formulating any IMS policy so that the message is not lost. However, most good policies written for quality, OH&S or environment will have addressed many of the above points and extending the scope may not be too difficult in such cases.

Those that have not developed and implemented any formal management system will need to approach an integrated policy in stages. If you are starting with little in place then it is suggested you do not try to write an elaborate policy at this stage. The time to write the policy is after the ISR and then revise it as necessary, notably after future management reviews.

The initial policy might therefore be drafted along the following lines:

> XYZ recognizes its responsibility to its customers, society, workforce, etc. and is committed to satisfying their needs. In order to meet this requirement XYZ will produce a fully developed policy and an IMS within (say), 6 months. This draft policy will then be reviewed and improved to reflect the organization's measures for controlling its risks (covered by the scope of the system).
>
> The organization is committed to meeting legal requirements and providing adequate resources to fulfil its policy obligations and will communicate to all relevant interested parties.

For those with established policies the approach should be to compare the wording of their policy against the points made above and also the respective policy requirements of ISO 9001:2000, ISO 14001:2004, BS OHSAS 18001:2007, etc. as appropriate. The generic policy of PAS 99, 4.2 will cover most of the needs as the main thrust is common in all such policies. However, specific clauses may need to be added to reflect the particular needs of one or more of the disciplines embraced within the IMS:

a) is appropriate to the organization's activities, products and services
The statement made should be relevant to the size and complexity of the organization. It needs to reflect the risks that the organization has to control in order to satisfy the expectations of all interested parties.

b) includes a commitment to comply with all relevant legal and other requirements to which the organization subscribes and to continually improve the effectiveness of the management system
This means there must be a commitment to meet internal policies, regulatory requirements, etc. that may apply to your product or service whether they relate to quality, environment or OH&S, etc. It equally applies to any commitment given to an interested party such as the customer, neighbours and/or employees.

c) provides a framework for establishing and reviewing objectives
The aim of this clause is to ensure the continued relevance of the policy statement. It seeks to demonstrate that there is a commitment to achieve an objective, for example, to improve the employees' working conditions.

d) is communicated to all persons working for or on behalf of the organization
It is essential that the policy commitment is communicated, presented and delivered in such a fashion that everyone working for the organization or on its behalf clearly understands and recognizes the organization's commitment to the statement.

e) is regularly reviewed for continuing suitability
Policies are live documents and need to be reviewed in the light of changes to the organization, for example, any new management standards adopted or changes in scope.

The following checklist will help you assess your policy statement and level of commitment. Any 'no' responses will need to be addressed before the policy is finalized and issued.

CHECKLIST

	Yes	No
Is your organization committed to its IMS covering XYZ in its entirety?	❑	❑
Is there someone in top management who has been given responsibility for seeing the system fully implemented and operational?	❑	❑
Does management take an active interest in monitoring the system and its performance?	❑	❑
Is your policy appropriate to the size of the organization?	❑	❑
Is your policy appropriate to the activities, products and services of your organization?	❑	❑
Does the policy commit the organization to comply with all relevant legal and other requirements?	❑	❑
Does the policy commit the organization to continually improve performance?	❑	❑
Does the policy provide a framework for establishing and reviewing objectives?	❑	❑
Does the organization commit to communicate the policy to all persons working for or on behalf of the organization?	❑	❑
Does the organization commit to a regular review of the continued suitability of the policy?	❑	❑
Have you addressed the specific policy issues of quality, etc.?	❑	❑

As the policy is being developed, attempts should be made to include input from appropriate interested parties. The policy needs to be realistic and the organization needs to assure itself that its claims can be achieved. If a vision or mission statement exists then the policy needs to refer to it and be consistent with it.

The policy should not make dogmatic statements. It would be unwise, for instance, to claim that the 'organization will never have a defect or an accident'. Neither should it try to distance itself from its responsibilities.

Statements such as 'we will make sure all employees have the common sense not to have accidents' are not appropriate!

Policy documentation and presentation

The policy needs to be focused on the requirements of the interested parties. Although there may be many parties who will rightly have access to the policy, it is important to recognize that the employees need to own it. If they cannot read and comprehend it and do not believe in it, it will serve little purpose. This situation can cause a dilemma. A very simple policy may be criticized by a sophisticated non-governmental organization that fights for the environment, yet a comprehensive policy may be difficult for the workforce to comprehend. In the final analysis the stakeholders are interested in output and not in glossy policies that do not deliver.

The policy statement should be kept simple and short, preferably on one sheet of A4 paper. For those who need further information, supplementary notes on the policy or commitments and how they are to be achieved can be provided as back-up information.

An example of an actual policy statement is given in Appendix 5.

Specific additional requirements of particular standards – management system policy

In addition to the elements of PAS 99, 4.2, provision needs to be made to meet the specific requirements of individual management system standards. Depending on the country/countries of operation and the nature of the product/services provided, the policy may need to cover local legal requirements and/or governmental regulations.

ISO 9001:2000

You may need to include specific issues/aspects such as the requirements of the EU Medical Devices Directive, or other statutory or regulatory requirements or industry codes of practice. You may also need to include specifications for methods, tests, etc. and other conditions of contract.

ISO 14001:2004

4.2 Policy –
the policy must be documented, implemented and maintained and be available to the public. (4.2)
There needs to be a commitment to continual improvement and the prevention of pollution. (4.2b)

BS OHSAS 18001:2007

1.2 Policy
The policy must be documented, implemented and maintained.
There is a need to communicate the policy to all persons working under the control of the organization with the intent that they are made aware of their individual OH&S obligations.
The policy must include a commitment to prevention of injury and ill health.

Reference should always be made to the relevant standards to ensure that the specific requirements are met. It should be remembered that just meeting the requirements of PAS 99 will not satisfy the specific requirements of the individual standards; it just provides an alignment of those that are common.

5. Planning

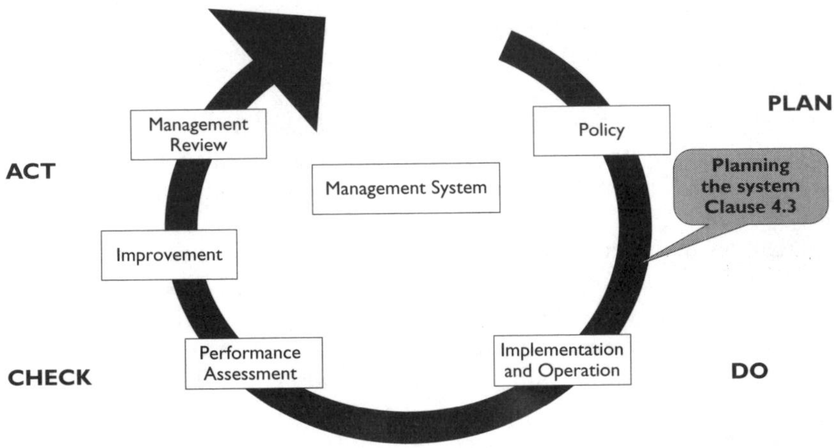

Figure 5.1

Identification and evaluation of aspects, impacts and risks

The organization shall establish, implement and maintain (a) procedure(s):

a) to identify the aspects of its activities, products and services relevant to the scope of the management system;

b) to evaluate the risks to the organization by determining and recording those aspects that have or can have a significant impact (i.e. significant aspects).

The organization shall ensure that the significant aspects are considered when establishing, implementing and maintaining its management system. (4.3.1)

Identification of aspects

Operational aspects

In any process there will be certain features designed to produce a desired outcome, and on which the result is dependent. Obvious examples in the quality field would be the quality and timeliness of material supplies or the capabilities of production equipment. These features are described as 'aspects'. If they are not controlled the desired outcome will not be achieved. The effect that an aspect could have on the outcome is described as an 'impact'.

In the first instance at least the aspects that need to be identified are those that are broadly covered by the scope of the IMS. However, it would obviously be foolish if issues that might give rise to significant impacts in other disciplines not under current review were ignored to the disadvantage of the organization. Using a checklist like the one shown in Table 5.1 could be helpful in making sure all aspects are covered. The particular headings used would depend, of course, on the scope of the IMS.

Table 5.1

Date **Reviewers**

Process and/or Product	Quality aspect	Environmental/ Waste aspect	Health aspect	Safety aspect
Input A				
Input B				
Input C				
Operation D				
Operation E				
Operation F				
Output G				
Output H				
Output I				
etc.				

Alternatively, you could use a set of questions to stimulate the evaluation, as in Table 5.2, which poses questions in respect of each product or service for a quality and environmental management system.

Table 5.2

Question	No	Yes	Details
During the input stage is there anything that might significantly affect the quality of the output?			
During the input stage is there anything that might significantly affect the environment?			
During the output stage is there anything that might significantly affect the quality?			
During the output stage is there anything that might significantly affect the environment?			

Business risks

Ideally, an organization will have identified its corporate risks and hence those that need to be controlled by the IMS, as highlighted in Chapter 2.

Identification of legal and other requirements

> The organization shall establish, implement and maintain (a) procedure(s) to determine the legal requirements relating to its activities, products and services that are relevant to the scope of the management system and take them into account when establishing, implementing and maintaining the management system. (4.3.2)

This area will not apply equally to all organizations and will very much depend on the country of operation and the disciplines embraced within the IMS. The areas to consider are:

- international conventions;
- national laws and regulations;
- local laws;
- industry codes of practice;
- society requirements.

Prioritizing aspects

There are no right or wrong ways of prioritizing aspects or risks. The methodologies proposed in ISO 14004:2004 and BS 8800:2004 are just some of many approaches. As stated above, it is good practice, if not essential, to work with personnel directly involved in the processes, both to identify and to prioritize the aspects. The process set out below is a convenient starting point.

Here again there is benefit in using a common approach across all management areas if it does not conflict with well-established processes. The use of a simple matrix like the one shown in Figure 5.2, as a first pass, helps to keep the effort proportionate to the risk and avoids excessive attention to one discipline at the expense of other equally important aspects in other disciplines.

Risk has two dimensions: likelihood and consequence. The risk of the aspect having a significant impact depends on the likelihood of the event happening and the consequence.

Matrices such as the one in Figure 5.2 are commonly used for OH&S and sometimes for ranking in environmental management. 'Consequence' needs to be considered in a number of lights depending on the discipline. 'Significant' in quality terms might mean a product recall, for instance; in environmental terms it might mean a major toxic spillage or loss of resource.

Using the matrix makes it possible to identify as a group those processes, or stages of a process, that could cause a significant quality defect, lead to ill health or a serious accident, a major environmental incident or shortage of material. The method used to identify the aspects and prioritization should be recorded/documented in some manner and those aspects that are considered significant should be listed.

Actions to deal with the significant aspects need to be considered in the light of:

- the number of significant aspects;
- the likelihood of immediate serious harm in the absence of action;
- financial loss;
- regulatory action;
- business opportunity;
- shareholder pressure;
- other stakeholder pressure;
- reputation issues.

It is obvious that some will need to be addressed urgently whilst others can be dealt with over a period of time. If, for instance, emission controls mean that new plant has to be installed, then an investment plan, etc. will need to be developed and the total time involved may be many months or years.

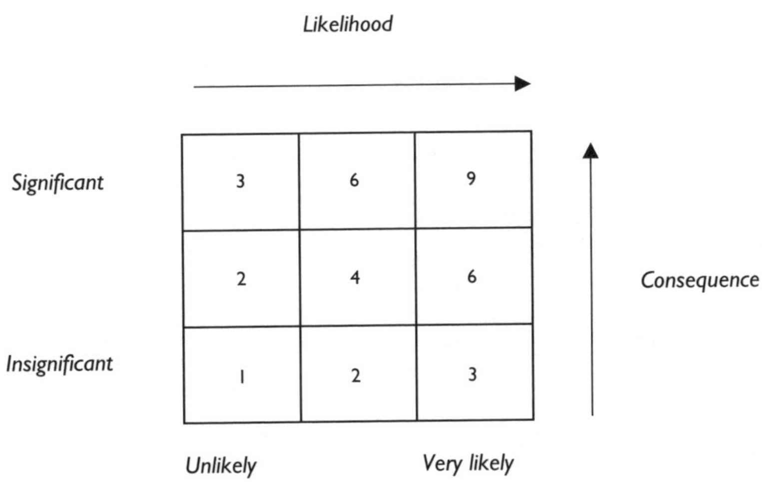

Figure 5.2

If you want to gain commitment for the new IMS then you should try to identify at least one aspect that can be tackled at an early stage, which heavily involves the workforce, and which gains their commitment.

Contingency planning

> The organization shall establish, document and maintain (a) procedure(s) for identifying and responding to any unplanned event, potential emergency or disaster. This procedure(s) shall seek to prevent or mitigate the consequences of any such occurrence and consider the continuity of the business operations. (4.3.3)

Although this element is not a very visible component of ISO 9001:2000 it is a key element of ISO 14001:2004 and BS OHSAS 18001:2007, where it is entitled 'emergency preparedness and response'. However, ISO 9001:2000 covers the requirement for preventive action and also recognizes the need for product recall, which could be an emergency situation where the prospects were potentially catastrophic.

The organization needs to consider the whole range of its activities, including its products and services, to determine if there are situations, no matter how unlikely, that it should plan to mitigate. As with other aspects the likelihood and consequences need to be established to ensure a measured response (see Figure 5.2).

The likelihood of being struck by an asteroid and the provisions needed to defend against it are such that it will not be worthy of consideration for most organizations. Other emergencies arise all too frequently. Every day some organization is destroyed by fire, flood or other disaster at their premises or at those of an essential supplier; a major customer fails; or civil unrest endangers material supplies. If these possibilities have not been anticipated the organization may well be endangered if for no other reason than it cannot meet its obligations to its customers.

> A large project involving the construction and operation of a road vehicle transportation system through a rail tunnel evaluated the risk of a fire arising in the tunnel.
>
> The initial risk assessment suggested at least once in 100 years. This indicated that the fire was as likely to arise in the first year of operation as in the 99th. Provision was therefore made accordingly.
>
> In the event there was a serious fire in the Channel Tunnel. The procedures were not implemented fully due to inadequate staff training and only by good fortune was serious loss of life avoided.

> An airliner struck a piece of debris on the runway on take-off. This caused a tyre to burst and the fragments punctured the fuel tanks, resulting in a fire that caused the deaths of all on board.
>
> The danger of such debris was well recognized, but these consequences had not been foreseen. All similar aircraft were withdrawn from service until the design had been modified to make the fuel tanks less vulnerable.

There are no rights or wrongs in establishing whether arrangements need to be put in place to control or mitigate the risk. It is a matter for judgement and evaluation by top management, but to make no provision for fire outbreak would be irresponsible in most situations. One way of bringing this matter the appropriate amount of attention is to use the checklist below.

CHECKLIST

	Yes	No
Has a list of potential emergency situations been compiled?	❑	❑
Has every senior manager been consulted and asked to suggest additions to the list?	❑	❑
Has each potential emergency situation been considered and:	❑	❑
a) the consequences documented?	❑	❑
b) the likelihood of the occurrence (and hence the risk) assessed?	❑	❑
c) categorized as: 1) high risk 2) acceptable 3) negligible or insignificant?	❑	❑
Has each situation in category 1) been further assessed and:	❑	❑
a) have the measures to prevent the occurrence or to mitigate the consequences been assessed?	❑	❑

b) have decisions been taken to implement such measures, a timetable agreed and responsibility allocated?	❑	❑
c) have recovery procedures been identified for each emergency?	❑	❑
d) has managerial responsibility been allocated for the implementation of these procedures if the emergency arises?	❑	❑
e) have the immediate procedures been discussed and cleared with external agencies such as the emergency services, environmental and OH&S authorities?	❑	❑
f) have recovery plans been discussed with other external bodies affected, e.g. suppliers, insurers?	❑	❑
Have methods been devised for testing plans for business continuity following an emergency situation and:	❑	❑
a) have procedures been issued?	❑	❑
b) is testing carried out regularly?	❑	❑
c) has management responsibility been allocated to ensure that these tests are carried out and the faults assessed?	❑	❑

The task is not only to prevent or mitigate an 'emergency' but also to ensure a quick recovery so that your services are restored for customers or production can resume with minimal delay.

Objectives

> The organization shall establish objectives, taking into account its significant aspects, legal obligations, other applicable requirements and its commitment to continual improvement when implementing its policy. These objectives shall be measurable. (4.3.4.1)
>
> The organization shall establish, implement and maintain (a) programme(s) for achieving its objectives. (4.3.4.2)

Determining objectives

The way the objectives are determined for the IMS is up to the organization. Objectives can be determined from the policy, the aspects list, brainstorming or the ISR. The objectives should be SMART:

- Specific;
- Measurable;
- Achievable;
- Realistic;
- Time based.

Once the objectives are set, the policy should be reviewed and may need revising. The objectives chosen should be relevant and realistically achievable. One way of setting meaningful objectives is to use 'action' words such as:

Introduce	'monthly management meetings'.
Implement	'an IMS'.
Improve	'the monitoring procedure'.
Reduce	'the number of failures'.
Increase	'the rate of training'.
Eliminate	'waste generated in … process'.

As with aspects, it is likely that there are many objectives that need to be achieved, but what is practical in terms of resources needs to be taken into account.

Some of the objectives may be subordinate to other objectives and may be embraced within an overall programme. What needs to be done is to determine those objectives that the organization can resource and that will give a good return.

Ideally, you will have involved employees in the aspect identification and prioritization programme and possibly to some extent in the ISR. The best way to gain their commitment is by seeking their advice and involvement in the selection of key objectives. Top management may also wish to select others or ones that require a heavy investment programme. Whatever the range of options, it is advisable to select one or more key objectives that have a large number of people involved. In some cases the objectives may need to be implemented at the operational level.

Objectives selection

The ISR, aspect identification and prioritization, policy statement and legal issues should help in determining those areas where controls need to be introduced, improved, maintained, etc. A set of action words such as those listed previously can be helpful.

You should not try to put everything right in one go. It is important to remember that you have to keep the business/service operational while improving it. An organization that delivers to superlative quality standards, reduces its environmental impacts to a minimum and protects all its workers from everything but goes bankrupt overnight is not really going to help any of the stakeholders. It is important to be realistic.

This process of objectives selection should have helped to prioritize the issues, and top management should agree on those to be addressed in the short to medium term. The aim should be to gain commitment to the system and the approach, and this will not be possible if the only objectives are long term.

Having selected a key objective it may be necessary to gather background information on the current situation in order to determine exactly where you are now. An objective such as 'reducing corrective actions within a target time of six months' is very laudable, but if the number of corrective actions per month is not known there is no way of demonstrating success or failure.

Gap analysis

If an organization already has in place quality and other systems, management needs to be conscious of the differences in scope that may exist between them. In general, quality systems will have been concerned only with the quality of the output – or possibly with only a specified part of the output. Health and safety, and environment, on the other hand, cannot be so restricted but extend throughout the organization and indeed beyond.

It is at this stage that the gap between what you have in place and what you need to deliver to meet your policy, objectives and effective aspect control measures will need to be established. The gap analysis will identify where there are missing 'boxes' or individual sub-elements in your existing arrangements or where you need to reinforce the arrangements.

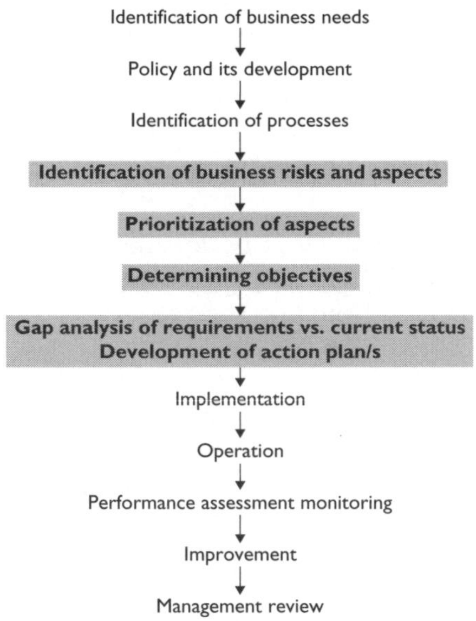

Figure 5.3

One way of identifying gaps is to produce a large checklist, such as the one shown in Table 5.3. The table gives just the generic headings but each of these may have specific aspects that need to be covered. For example, under 'health' you may instigate an objective (or policy) on dealing with noise-induced deafness; the policy section may then be an objective rather than a policy but the rest should follow the general format.

Organizational structure, roles, responsibilities and authorities

> The organization's top management shall appoint (a) specific management representative(s) who, irrespective of other responsibilities, shall have defined roles, responsibilities and authority for:
>
> a) ensuring that the management system is established, implemented and maintained in accordance with the

> requirements of this PAS and the management system standards/specifications to which the organization subscribes;
>
> b) reporting to top management on the performance of the management system for review, including recommendations for improvement. (4.3.5.1)
>
> The organization shall identify, document and communicate the roles, responsibilities and authorities of those involved in the management system and their interrelationships within the organization. (4.3.5.2)

It will be clear from the start that the success of the system and the timescale in which it is implemented depends on top management. Only if they are truly committed will it be implemented effectively and in a reasonable timescale. It is now a common, if not a legal, requirement in the country(ies) in which the organization operates, for top management to be held accountable for environmental and OH&S failures, which means a top manager will have these fields as one of his/her prime responsibilities. Recently the changes implemented by ISO 9001:2000 have taken this high ground and seek top management responsibility for quality management.

So the IMS needs a senior manager as its focus although operational issues may be handled at a lower level. This appointee needs to show real commitment and not be just a figurehead. To some extent the attitude on corporate governance will ensure this commitment. The organization should, as a matter of course, review the control of all its risks and the IMS should be the cornerstone of its risk control measures.

This commitment to the system as a formal control system is not sufficient in itself. The employees need to be committed as well and know the roles that they play. This means commitment has to be instilled from the top management down to all those involved in the effective and efficient operation of the IMS. This task and its importance should not be underestimated. An organization can experience a catastrophic problem from some minor task that is not even associated with the core activity. A junior employee turning a wrong tap, given poor directions or failing to act can be fatal.

Table 5.3

Requirements of PAS 99 Objective Aspect	**Quality**	**Health**	**Safety**	**Fire**	**Environ-ment**	**etc.**
Management system	Yes/No	Yes/No	Yes/No	Yes/No	Yes/No	Yes/No
Policy: policy and/or principles						
4.1 General requirements						
4.2 Management system policy						
4.3 Planning 4.3.1 Identification and evaluation of aspects, impacts and risks 4.3.2 Identification of legal and other requirements 4.3.3 Contingency planning 4.3.4 Objectives 4.3.5 Organizational structure, roles, responsibilities and authorities						
4.4 Implementation and operation 4.4.1 Operational control 4.4.2 Management of resources 4.4.3 Documentation requirements 4.4.4 Communication						
4.5 Performance assessment 4.5.1 Monitoring and measurement 4.5.2 Evaluation of compliance 4.5.3 Internal audit 4.5.4 Handling of nonconformities						

4.6 Improvement 4.6.1 General 4.6.2 Corrective, preventive and improvement action						
4.7 Management review 4.7.1 General 4.7.2 Input 4.7.3 Output						

Shipping disasters offer striking examples. The *Herald of Free Enterprise* sank at Zeebrugge because someone did not check that the bow doors were closed before the ship started out. The *Marchioness* was run down because a lookout on the *Bow Belle* failed to see it. The bulk carrier *Derbyshire* sank with all hands perhaps because a deck hatch had not been properly secured.

Hence, the identification of responsibilities and accountabilities, and the assessment of the skills and competencies needed, should be carried out carefully. A checklist to help you in this task is provided below.

CHECKLIST

	Yes	No
Has a top manager been appointed to be responsible for the implementation of the IMS throughout the organization?	❑	❑
Have all departments been informed about the appointment and the top-level commitment this implies?	❑	❑
Does every manager and every employee understand their role in the implementation of the system?	❑	❑
If not, are suitable steps being taken to make them aware?	❑	❑
Have the competencies required for each task been identified?	❑	❑
Are the competencies of each employee involved sufficient?	❑	❑
Have plans been made to make good any shortcoming – by training, staff transfer, etc.?	❑	❑

Has each manager a timed and measurable programme of phases in achievement?	❑	❑
Has a system been implemented for the reporting of progress?	❑	❑
Are arrangements in hand to make good any shortfall in the programme?	❑	❑
Have contractors been included in the programme where necessary?	❑	❑

Specific additional requirements of particular standards – planning

This is the most important section of all management systems. There are different approaches in all the standards/specifications. This book shows that there can be a unified approach but the reader needs to study the separate documents and support information to completely understand the requirements and the individual nuances applying to individual disciplines.

How you identify and prioritize aspects will very much depend on the sector in which you operate, the nature of the risks and any regulatory controls that apply. Remember also that the language used may be different. For instance the common approach in OH&S is to focus on 'hazards' and 'risks', which are roughly equivalent to 'aspect' and 'impact' in PAS 99; see ISO 14001 below.

ISO 9001:2000

5.4 Planning (especially roles and responsibility)
5.4.1 Quality objectives for product requirements
7.3 Design and development

ISO 14001:2004

4.3 Planning (especially the need to keep information up to date, and the means and time frame for objectives).

Note that this standard talks in terms of objectives and targets, this latter term not appearing in other standards.

The approach talks about aspects and the impacts – both positive and negative – and they are defined as follows:

Environmental aspect. The element of an organization's activities, products or services that can interact with the environment.

Note that a significant environmental aspect is one that has or can have a significant environmental impact.

Environmental impact. Any change to the environment, whether adverse or beneficial, wholly or partially resulting from an organization's environmental aspects.

There is little guidance as to how this might be achieved in ISO 14001 although more information can be obtained from ISO 14004 and books such as *Managing the Environment the ISO 14001 Way*.

ISO 14001 (Annex A, A.3.1) proposes:

> Although there is no single approach for identifying environmental aspects, the approach selected could for example consider
>
> a) emissions to air;
> b) releases to water;
> c) releases to land;
> d) use of raw materials and natural resources;
> e) use of energy;
> f) energy emitted, e.g. heat, radiation, vibration;
> g) waste and by-products; and
> h) physical attributes, e.g. size, shape, colour, appearance.

This process should consider normal operating conditions, shut-down and start-up conditions, as well as the realistic, potentially significant impacts associated with reasonably foreseeable or emergency situations. There is also a need to identify past activities and consider future plans as well as the current operation.

The process is intended to identify significant environmental aspects associated with activities, products or services, and is not intended to require a detailed life cycle assessment. Organizations do not have to evaluate each product, component or raw material input. They may select categories of activities, products or services to identify those aspects most likely to have a significant impact.

BS OHSAS 18001:2007

4.3 Planning

BS OHSAS 18001 breaks the identification of hazard and risk into two processes. 'Hazard' is defined as the 'source, situation or act with a potential for harm in terms of human injury or ill health, or a combination of these'. 'Risk' is defined as the 'combination of the likelihood of an occurrence of a hazardous event or exposure(s) and the severity of injury or ill health that can be caused by the event or exposure(s)'. 'Acceptable risk' is defined as 'risk that has been reduced to a level that can be tolerated by the organization having regard to its legal obligations and its own OH&S policy'.

The aim in OH&S is entirely preventive – to avoid ill health and accidents. In an ideal world all the situations would be assessed and those risks that were acceptable would be discounted. The other risks would be reviewed and control measures implemented where necessary. As an organization matures some 'acceptable' risks may be reconsidered to assess whether an improvement can be made and justified. BS OHSAS 18001:2007 requires a hierarchical approach in dealing with risks and insists that an organization manages itself as it changes and recognizes the risks arising.

Reference should always be made to the standard itself to ensure that the specific requirements are met.

6. Implementing and operating

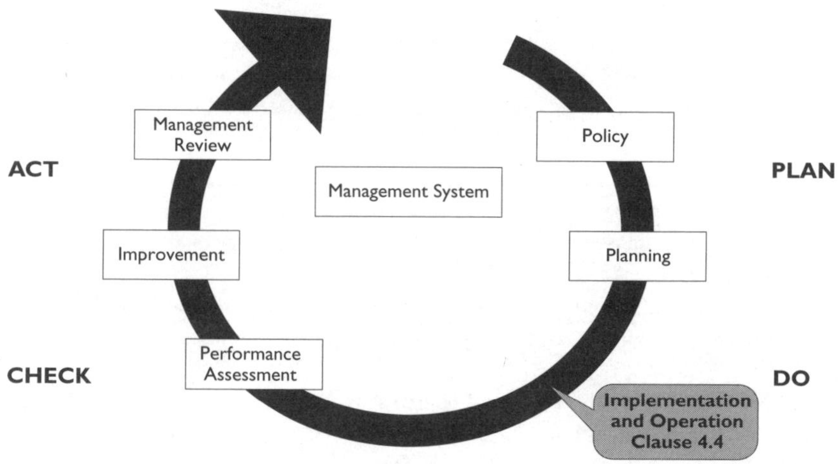

Figure 6.1

It is very unlikely that your organization has nothing in place and nothing to build on. Usually, apart from the normal operating procedures, some process has been implemented for invoicing, customer complaints, accident recording, contingency preparedness, etc. If these arrangements are working satisfactorily make sure you congratulate the parties involved and take them along with you in the implementation process. Remember, you need people on board to make the IMS work. There are many examples where excellent systems existed but the lack of commitment to them resulted in catastrophic failure.

So, use the expertise available. Find out what pitfalls people have encountered (or are encountering) and try to establish what will make it work.

A company with 60 employees was to be moved from the public sector to the private sector but had lost $0.8m in the first year of operation. Moreover in its second year it had lost $180k in the first two months; it had received many customer complaints; and had had a bad accident resulting in an initial claim of $50k against the organization. It had no systems for quality, environment or OH&S.

A change in management and cultural approach resulted in an embryonic IMS being developed and the profitability in the last 10 months of the financial year was $170k without any enforced redundancies and the loss of only two staff through natural wastage.

The workforce had committed to change because of the financial situation and their job security, and they significantly contributed to the provision of a better, more cost-effective service that was more environmentally sound and reduced OH&S risks.

A manufacturing company had an accident record such that it was reaching the point where it was uninsurable. Its quality records were also poor despite ISO 9001 registration.

Everyone in management knew about the legal requirements for OH&S and had 'excellent safety manuals', which they chose to ignore when meeting production schedules.

The board decided on a new 'cultural' approach to OH&S, downgrading the influence of mere legal compliance in favour of the need to avoid accidents/ill health and to promote the organization by greater effectiveness.

A one-week course for senior managers was embarked upon, focusing on the downside of failure with respect to human misery and the cost of production. Some managers stated on day one that they could not afford the time wasted on such a course! The managing director attended the first course after hearing of this and asked those who could not spare the time to be there to declare themselves! He made the point that he would seek replacements who could afford the time.

Subsequently those who had been most antagonistic took a keen interest and committed to the process.

The result was over a $1.5m per annum reduction in accident/ill health claims and a reduction in quality defects down to zero.

The organization committed itself to the implementation of risk control management systems similar to the IMS framework.

Operational control

> The organization shall ensure that the operations that are associated with significant aspects are carried out under specified conditions in order to meet the organization's policies and objectives as well as legal and other applicable requirements. (4.4.1)

The control measures necessary for meeting the policy, objectives, targets and aspect mitigation should have already been planned. Now these have to be implemented ensuring that the necessary processes, documents and resources are in place and there is a need to instigate the monitoring procedure to verify and validate that what should be happening really is happening.

To back up this stage, records should be kept.

Implementation of operational control measures

It is all very well determining the aspects and control measures, but there is also the need to plan for effective implementation. To begin with, consider the IMS policy, the objectives and targets stemming from the policy, and aspect control measures. You may for instance decide you want to reduce or control a particular waste or use of resource. Before these can be implemented we need to establish all the steps or stages where controls need to be implemented. In some cases, there will be a need to gather key information. There is no point in committing to reducing the waste in production process B or the number of incidents of employees with back problems in office C if there is no baseline so it is necessary to gather information and plan to meet the SMART objectives we have set.

By now the necessary resources will have been identified for implementation on the whole front. A chart of the various initiatives showing targets, resources, etc. is useful for identifying the key steps and deliverables.

Management of resources

Identification of resources

Having established the gaps and set your priorities, you will have some idea of what has to be done and the timescales needed to develop and implement the IMS.

More important in some ways is the matter of resources. There will always be financial limitations and possibly human resource factors (numbers, time and skill sets) that have to be taken into consideration. This may affect the order in which tasks are tackled.

This requires that you consider the day-to-day needs of operating the system together with those resources needed for implementing the control measures identified for the policy, objectives and aspects register. To some extent the assessment of needs can only be made after 'Implementation of operational control measures' (see above) and should obviously be closely linked with this stage.

As with so many of these planning stages the process must be regarded as iterative. You will not be able to achieve a comprehensive and accurate assessment on day one. There is nothing wrong with approximations, or even guesses, as long as it is remembered that this is what they are, and that they need to be refined as further information becomes available.

If there is to be only one management system then top management will be involved in establishing the system and ensuring that it delivers the objectives and targets. However, the day-to-day management of specific tasks or management programmes may primarily lie at different levels within the organization. It is for top management to identify or to establish a process for identifying the aspects and then for them to assign the resources necessary to achieve the objectives and targets. A checklist such at the one shown in Table 6.1 may be useful.

For instance it may be that the management of waste is one of the significant aspects. The day-to-day arrangements for this may well be at a very junior operational level in the organization. On the other hand a particular quality aspect may be under direct operational control at a very senior level.

It is up to top management to determine that there are adequate human, infrastructure and financial resources to meet the requirements of the policy and system and to continually improve its effectiveness.

When drawing up the plan for operational control the resource needs should be determined for the collective actions planned and hence the time frame and/or targets adjusted according to what is achievable. The identification of an individual or team responsible for delivering one objective will enable a focused approach to the targets.

Table 6.1

Operational Level	Responsibility		
	Top Management	Middle Management	Operational
Strategic	✓		
Strategic/management	✓	✓	
Strategic/management/operational	✓	✓	✓
Management		✓	
Management/operational		✓	✓
Operational			✓

Management of human resources

> The organization shall ensure that all people working for or on behalf of the organization are competent on the basis of appropriate education, training, skills and experience for the tasks assigned to them. (4.4.2.1)
>
> The organization shall:
>
> a) evaluate the effectiveness of the actions taken to ensure competence;
> b) ensure that its personnel are aware of the relevance and importance of their activities and how they contribute to the achievement of the objectives. (4.4.2.2)

It is a common mistake to assume that someone who has been trained is also competent. The fact that someone has passed their driving test for driving a car on a road does not mean they are competent to drive in a Formula 1 Grand Prix. It is equally true for a forklift truck drivers; even if they have taken a course and passed successfully, the employers may want to evaluate their proficiency when operating at their site before finally accepting them for this task. This evaluation may need to be repeated every few months/years depending on the circumstances.

> The continual training and testing of airline pilots is well known, but even in less high-profile activities regular training and testing may be necessary.
>
> Employees engaged to work on the railway track in the UK have to attend a special course lasting for a number of days concerning track safety.
>
> Subsequently, the workers have to pass a test on the subject matter before they are allowed to work on the track. Once a year they are reviewed.
>
> Such an approach is common in many other industries.

This point needs to be taken further. Should someone fail to undertake their duties correctly and this is observed during monitoring or auditing or results in a near miss incident, their competence may need to be reviewed. For example, there may be a number of physical reasons why an employee cannot perform to the desired standard: failing eyesight or hearing with age may necessitate a change in duties for the sake of safety as much as for the need to mitigate errors, etc.

It is obviously important to explain to employees what needs to be done and how they should do it. Equally, it is important for them to understand the importance of their role and what could happen if they did not undertake the task in the prescribed manner.

Management of other resources

> The organization shall determine, provide and maintain the resources and infrastructure needed to achieve its objectives. (4.4.2.3)

a) buildings, workspace and associated utilities
The provision of infrastructure to meet the needs is an obvious requirement but it is sometimes forgotten that buildings, work areas and support facilities need regular maintenance, replacement, cleaning, etc. You need to allow for the reviewing of the infrastructure in the broadest sense, bearing in mind technology changes, workplace expectations, changes in workload and reliability, consistency and other quality aspects.

b) process equipment (both hardware and software)
This point about infrastructure is particularly important in respect of hardware and software, which date very quickly. Reliance on computers increases the risk of accidental loss of data, which can have serious

consequences. Information security may well be something that you want to include in your IMS (see ISO 27001). A book on this topic is included in this series (*IMS: Information Security*).

c) supporting services (such as transport or communication hardware)
Transport services are sometimes not seen as a core issue. However, they can impact on the environment through poor environmental specification, and OH&S issues can arise related to transport – driver hours, carriage of dangerous loads, insufficient training, the type of vehicles used or poor maintenance.

> At first sight, using an electric powered vehicle seems an environmentally sound option. However, you need to consider the emissions arising at the source of the power generation and the efficiency in converting it to the energy used in transport. Coal-fired power stations emit up to 1,000 g of CO_2 per kilowatt-hour produced.
>
> The needs of the customer with respect to speed, quality, etc. also need to be considered.

Communication or its absence is often an organizational weakness; this will be addressed below. Suffice it to say that it is a key element for ensuring effective operational control, and one aspect is the infrastructure for delivering communication.

Documentation requirements

> The management system documentation shall include:
>
> a) a description of the scope of the management system, including the management systems standards/ specifications subscribed to;
> b) statements of the organization's policies and objectives;
> c) a system manual describing the main elements of the management system and their interaction, including common policies, processes and procedures and references to related documents;
> d) the documented procedures and records that are required by this PAS and the management system

standards/specifications to which the organization subscribes;

e) documents determined as necessary by the organization to ensure the effective planning, operation and control of its processes. (4.4.3.1)

It has been said before but bears repeating: 'The documentation should support and not drive the system'.

The requirements listed in 4.4.3.1 are self-explanatory but caution is essential. An organization with three manuals for each of the disciplines of quality, environment, and health and safety (policy and arrangements, procedures, and work instructions in three areas) will have obviously failed if its IMS output is nine manuals, or three manuals that are three times as thick as the manual in any previous discipline. As a significant proportion of the systems should typically be common (see Appendix 2), this clearly would be a failure and would not result in an effective or efficient IMS.

Many organizations have found great benefit in using a flow chart or charts to minimize the volume of paperwork. Such an approach, in a paper or electronic format, is far more accessible to employees. It enables users to find their way around the system very efficiently.

The management system documentation can be computer based. This makes updating easier and can ensure that no obsolete documents are in use, but all employees must have ready access to the information that they need, and approval processes (see 4.4.3.3) need to be carefully designed.

You need to bear in mind that the different standards may require different procedures for documentation. This depends in part on the legal requirements that may apply to the quality or safety of goods, environmental and OH&S control measures, or OH&S reporting and recording requirements.

The system manual

The normal requirements of management system documentation apply here: you need documented statements on policy and objectives, a manual describing the working of the system and integrated work instructions.

It is recognized that there is interaction between the processes of the management system and this is required to be identified and described. Again, the use of flow diagrams will serve this function.

Document control

Documents required by the management system shall be controlled. (4.4.3.2)

The organization shall establish, implement and maintain (a) documented procedure(s) to define the controls needed to:

a) approve documents for adequacy prior to issue;
b) review and update and re-approve documents as necessary;
c) ensure that changes and current revision status of documents are identified;
d) ensure that relevant versions of applicable documents are available at points of use;
e) ensure that documents remain legible and readily identifiable;
f) ensure that documents of external origin are identified and their distribution controlled;
g) prevent the unintended use of obsolete documents, and to apply suitable identification to them if they are retained for any purpose. (4.4.3.3)

The important point to note here is that there may be legal requirements on the control of some documentation and those may need to be satisfied over and above the system requirements. Should this be the case it may be more efficient to adopt the more stringent requirement throughout unless this is over-bureaucratic and burdensome.

Control of records

Records shall be established, documented and maintained to provide evidence of conformity to requirements and of the effective operation of the management system. (4.4.3.4)

The organization shall establish, implement and maintain (a) documented procedure(s) to define the controls needed for the identification, storage, protection, retrieval, retention and disposal of records. (4.4.3.5)

It has become increasingly apparent in a number of fields that some records need to be kept for a very long period, for example design plans, records of employees' exposure to workplace risks, and environmental emissions. Other records need only be kept for a short time. You need to carefully review the records produced and decide what needs to be kept for what period of time. This will enable processes to be developed for the control of records that are appropriate to your specific needs. This is an area where different arrangements may need to be applied to satisfy the individual disciplines covered by the scope of the integrated system.

Communication

> The organization shall establish, implement and maintain effective arrangements for:
>
> a) internal communication amongst the various levels and functions of the organization;
> b) receiving, recording and responding to relevant communications from interested parties. (4.4.4.1)
>
> The organization shall decide whether to actively communicate with external interested parties and shall document its decision. (4.4.4.2)
>
> If the decision is to communicate with external interested parties, the organization shall establish and implement (a) method(s) for communication. (4.4.4.3)

One of the most common complaints made about an organization is its communication arrangements. Often there are complaints of too little communication or even none at all. However, too much communication can be nearly as bad. Some organizations have totally failed in OH&S management by communicating too much, thinking that management has fulfilled its duty by passing on to employees everything that is received on the subject.

You need to strike the right balance. The communication from top management should be appropriate to the needs of the employee so that he or she can carry out the task in the desired manner in terms of quality, environment, OH&S, etc. and understand the reasons. Equally, there needs to be an efficient system of communication in the opposite direction from the employee to top management. In the revised standards the intent is that employees should be actively encouraged to be involved and a true process of consultation to be in place.

When considering who is an 'external interested party' with whom you should be communicating, it is essential to remember that the workforce is an interested party that may act partly through external bodies, e.g. trade unions. Similarly, the arrangements for communicating with suppliers and contractors who have a significant impact on the organization's performance should be formalized.

Specific additional requirements of particular standards – implementation and operation

In addition to the elements of PAS 99, provision needs to be made to meet the specific requirements of individual management system standards.

ISO 9001:2000

5.5 Responsibility, authority and communication (especially the appointment of a management representative, 5.5.2).
5.5.3 Internal communication.
6.2 Human resources (especially records of training, etc. 6.2.2).
6.4 Work environment.
7.2 Customer-related processes.
7.3 Design and development.
7.4 Purchasing.
7.5 Production and service provision.
7.6 Control of monitoring and measuring devices.
8 Measurement, analysis and improvement (especially 8.2 Monitoring and measurement).

ISO 14001:2004

4.4 Implementation and operation (especially the appointment of a management representative (4.4.1) and the specific requirement that personnel must be aware of the potential consequences of departure from specified procedures (4.4.2)).

BS OHSAS 18001:2007

4.4 Implementation and operation, especially:
4.4.1 Management responsibility and the appointment of management representative;
4.4.3.2 Participation and consultation;
4.4.6 Operational control;
4.4.7 Emergency preparedness and response.

Reference should always be made to the relevant standards to ensure that the specific requirements are met.

7. Performance assessment

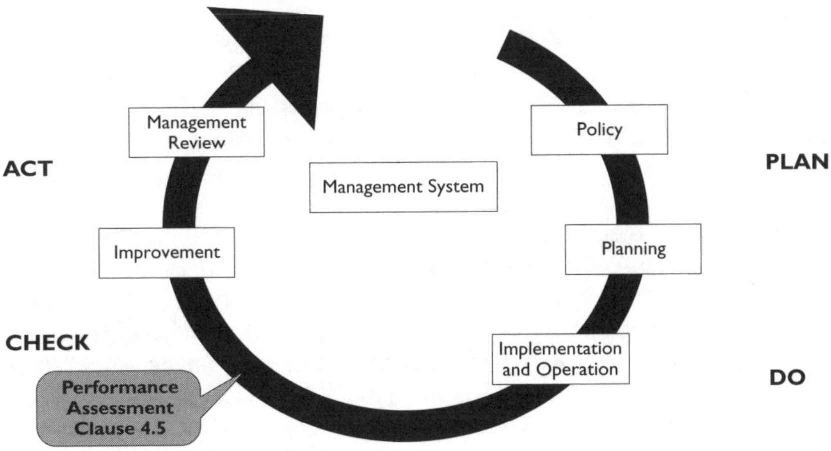

Figure 7.1

There is a requirement to improve performance over time. This policy objective requires a mechanism for measuring, monitoring, auditing, analysing and dealing with nonconformities.

Monitoring and measurement

> The organization shall carry out monitoring and measurement in order to determine the extent to which applicable requirements are being met. This shall include the recording of information to track performance of relevant operational controls and to evaluate conformance with the organization's objectives and the ability of the processes to achieve planned results. (4.5.1)

The old adage 'If you can't measure it you can't manage it' is well founded. If you have not determined how many of your products fall into the category of needing some remedial action after production to make them fit for sale, it is no use setting a target of '50 per cent reduction in the number of reworked items'. It is necessary to establish baselines against which performance improvements can be assessed/measured.

Some factors can be more difficult to measure. For instance, it can be difficult to quantify a customer saying, 'They seem to be a good company'. In such cases it may be necessary to use attitude surveys.

To achieve the objectives, you will need to have established the characteristics you will measure when drawing up your plans to meet them.

This is self-evident, but again emphasizes the need to gather baseline information before starting to implement a plan. It may become obvious that the plan is going awry or that the characteristics selected for monitoring are inadequate. This information is vital and should form part of the feedback loop into the review process so that the system can be improved accordingly. It is important to put checks in at various stages of the programme so that any shortfall can be detected and rectified.

Ideally the system should be implemented so that the performance can be effectively evaluated. There is a need to be proactive rather than reactive, and to continually improve. There are many models that can be used for this purpose; the one given in ISO 14031:2000 is very simple and can be used generically. It was adopted in the environmental field for ISO and recognized the need for guidance in establishing an approach for evaluating performance. ISO 14031 is a useful tool that has been primarily developed for those seeking to improve their environmental performance, but the methodology has far greater application. The terminology and examples used for management performance indicators (MPIs) and operational performance indicators (OPIs) have a generic application and can equally be used for quality and OH&S, bearing in mind the different stakeholder requirements. Obviously the environmental condition indicators (ECIs) only apply to environmental issues, but indicators of performance for the other disciplines are possible.

A checklist for performance monitoring is given below.

CHECKLIST

Examples of proactive monitoring data

- Progress in achieving the plans and objectives that have been set ❑
- Results of attitude surveys of employees' perceptions of management commitment to IMS ❑
- Appointment of a director/senior manager for IMS ❑
- Appointment, where necessary, of specialist staff ❑
- Progress on publishing an IMS policy ❑
- Progress on communicating the IMS policy ❑
- Progress on training personnel on the IMS system ❑
- Monitoring the effectiveness of IMS training ❑
- Progress in completing the risk assessment programme ❑
- Monitoring compliance with risk controls ❑
- Monitoring compliance with statutory requirements ❑
- Monitoring the number and effectiveness of IMS tours, inspections/surveys ❑
- Monitoring the number of staff suggestions for IMS improvements ❑
- Monitoring staff attitudes to risks and risk controls ❑
- Monitoring staff understanding of risks and risk controls ❑
- Progress on completing IMS audits ❑
- Progress on implementing IMS audit recommendations ❑
- Monitoring the frequency and effectiveness of IMS committee meetings ❑

Monitoring the frequency and effectiveness of staff IMS briefings	❑
Progress on IMS specialist reports	❑
Progress on implementing action on complaints and suggestions	❑
Examples of reactive monitoring data	
Reported near-misses	❑
Reported damage-only incidents	❑
Reportable dangerous occurrences	❑
Lost-time accidents – when at least one work shift (or other time period) is lost by a person as a result of an accident or injury	❑
Reportable accidents involving absence from work for more than three days	❑
Reportable major incidents	❑
Sickness absence – employee absences due to illness (occupationally-related or non-occupationally related)	❑
Complaints made, for example by members of the public	❑
Criticisms made by regulatory agency staff	❑
Regulatory agency enforcement action	❑

Many tools are available worldwide for evaluating performance including the EFQM Excellence Model, the Baldrige criteria and assessment processes, and variations on these.

The 'interested parties' vary slightly depending on the discipline, but there are many common to all three subject areas.

In essence, the model shown in Figure 7.2 simplistically sees an organization as being comprised of two elements: management and operation. Each of these interacts with interested parties in a number of ways. The role of management is seen as one of making strategic/business decisions whilst the operation strives to achieve maximum day-to-day efficiency and effectiveness with the tools/systems that it currently has available to it. Management's interaction with interested parties may lead to MPIs being introduced and applied that are communicated as actions to the operational functions. At the operational level these may be incorporated into OPIs.

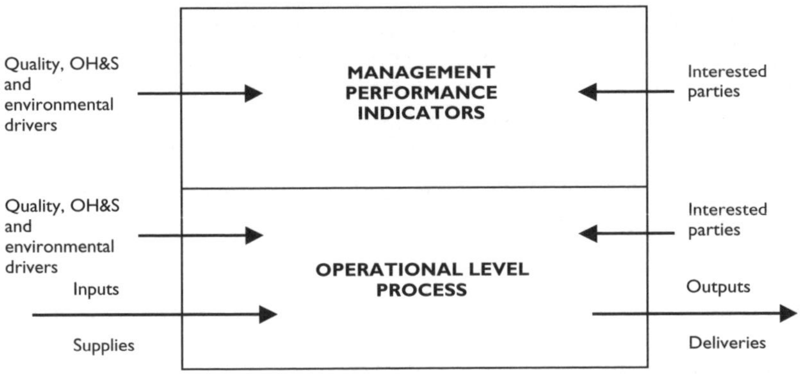

Figure 7.2

The processes within the company at the operational level receive corporate direction on the way they strategically deal with quality, environment, and OH&S. There will always be local issues that will need to be directly responded to at local level on a day-to-day basis.

If one considers the above controls and interactions in three parts, then a process for establishing performance criteria emerges.

The 'ambient conditions' with respect to quality, environment and OH&S drivers will determine the MPIs and OPIs.

Some of the generic headings for MPIs and OPIs are given below.

Implementation of policies and programmes

- number of achieved objectives;
- number of organizational units achieving objectives;
- degree of implementation of specified codes of management or operating practice;
- number of employees participating in improvement programmes;

- number of employees who have obtained reward and recognition in comparison to the total number of employees who participated in the programme;
- number of employees trained versus the number that need training;
- number of contracted individuals trained;
- levels of knowledge obtained by training participants;
- number of improvement suggestions from employees;
- results of employee surveys on their knowledge of the organization's management control issues;
- number of suppliers and contractors questioned about management performance issues;
- number of contracted service providers with an implemented or certified management system.

Conformance

- degree of compliance with regulations;
- degree of conformance of service providers with requirements and expectations specified by the organization in contracts;
- time to respond to or correct adverse incidents;
- number of, or costs attributable to, fines and penalties;
- number and frequency of specific activities (e.g. audits);
- number of audits completed versus planned;
- number of audit findings or adverse findings per period;
- frequency of review of operating procedures.

Some initial objectives can be established using these performance indicators in the ISR process and implementation programmes can be set up as appropriate. This can lead to the development of specific key performance indicators (KPIs) to enable the organization to show continually improved performance.

Financial performance

- costs (operational and capital) that are associated with a product or process's aspects;
- return on investment for improvement projects;

- savings achieved through reductions in resource usage, low direct waste, prevention of pollution, accidents, ill health or waste recycling, etc.;
- sales revenue attributable to a new product or a by-product designed to meet performance or design objectives;
- research and development funds applied to projects with performance improvement;
- liabilities that may have a material impact on the financial status of the organization.

Stakeholder relations

- number of enquiries or comments about business risk-related matters;
- number of press reports on the organization's performance;
- number of educational programmes or materials provided for the stakeholders;
- favourability ratings from stakeholder surveys.

Evaluation of compliance

> The organization shall carry out periodic evaluations of compliance with legal requirements that are relevant to the scope of the management system and record the results. (4.5.2)

For a management system to be truly effective and efficient it needs to identify opportunities for improvement and implement appropriate actions. As stated previously the aim is to be proactive not reactive. A reactive management system as the main thrust means that there is a well-oiled machine for recovery from failures, disasters, etc. The ideal arrangement is to identify shortfalls and to anticipate potential problems by being proactive. This should meet all stakeholder requirements as well as ensuring that all legal requirements are met. As a safeguard it is necessary periodically to review the legal and other requirements that the organization is subject to, to ensure that no infringements arise.

Internal audit

> The organization shall establish and maintain an audit programme for conducting periodic management system audits to determine whether or not the management system:
>
> a) conforms to planned arrangements including the requirements of this PAS and other management system standards/specifications to which the organization subscribes (see 4.3);
> b) has been properly implemented and maintained, and is being adhered to. (4.5.3.1)
>
> The audit programme, including any schedule, shall be based on the significance of management system aspects, the organization's risks, the organization's performance and the results of previous audits. (4.5.3.2)
>
> The audit arrangements shall cover the scope, frequency, methodologies and competencies, as well as the responsibilities and requirements for conducting audits and reporting results. (4.5.3.3)
>
> The selection of auditors and the conduct of audits shall ensure objectivity and the impartiality of the audit process. (4.5.3.4)

The auditing process is frequently misunderstood, probably because of its bookkeeping and accountancy associations. It is an essential part of any system simply to make sure that the system is working. When the management review comes to consider whether the system is producing the results that are needed, it is necessary to be sure that the system is being followed. If one cannot be certain of this, it is not possible to judge whether any failures are due to shortcomings in the system itself or merely that the system is not being followed.

Audits therefore have a number of distinct functions in answering the following questions:

- Is the system being followed in all respects?
- If not, is this due to staff deficiencies in:
  - competence?
  - management?
  - training?

- or system deficiencies in:
  - inadequate definitions?
  - inadequate design?

Failures to follow the system are as often the result of deficiencies in the system as inadequacies in the staff, and should be regarded as opportunities for improving the system.

Any organization with a management system in place should have an established process for internal audit. The audit requirements of all management systems are very similar and hence the process for an integrated audit should be based upon the existing arrangements if they are satisfactory.

The following checklist covers the main requirements.

CHECKLIST

	Yes	No
Are periodic audits of the integrated system taking place?	❑	❑
Do they cover all parts of the system?	❑	❑
Is the frequency of the audit determined by the risk?	❑	❑
Are those conducting the audit competent in all the fields that they will encounter?	❑	❑
Are they independent of the areas that they are auditing?	❑	❑
Are the audit results communicated to all relevant personnel?	❑	❑
Are they used as the basis for corrective action?	❑	❑
Are such actions recorded?	❑	❑
Are all audit results and corrective actions reported in suitable format for management review meetings?	❑	❑
Are audit procedures regularly reviewed with the objective of continual improvement?	❑	❑

The regular auditing of the system is one of the main drivers for successful operational improvement. Its importance is such that there is a separate book on the subject in this series (*IMS: Continual Improvement through Auditing*).

Handling nonconformities

> Where nonconformities are identified they shall be corrected and action taken to mitigate their impact (see 4.6). (4.5.4)

This is discussed in greater detail in Chapter 8.

Specific additional requirements of particular standards – performance assessment

In addition to the elements of PAS 99, provision needs to be made to meet the specific requirements of individual management system standards as follows.

ISO 9001:2000

8.3 Control of nonconforming product.
8.4 Analysis of data.

ISO 14001:2004

Documented procedures are required, specifically for the periodic evaluation of legal compliance (4.5.2) and recording the results.

BS OHSAS 18001:2007

4.5 Checking (especially incident investigation, etc.).
4.5.2 The organization is required to keep records of the results of periodic evaluations of compliance.

Reference should always be made to the relevant standard itself to ensure that the specific requirements are met.

8. Improvement

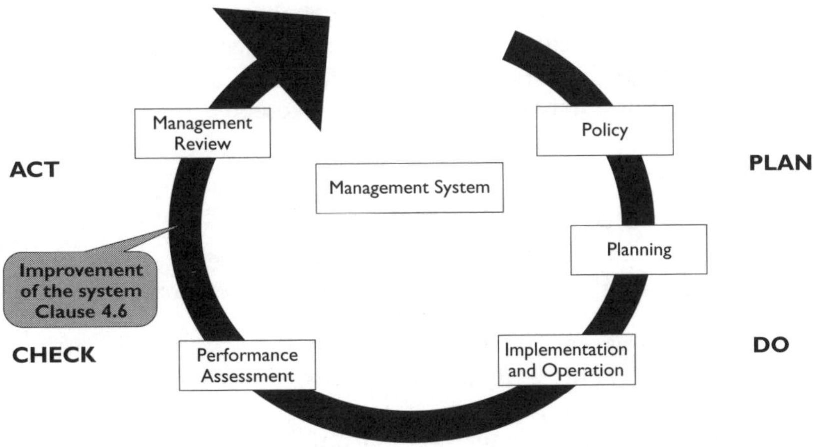

Figure 8.1

General

The organization shall continually improve the effectiveness of the management system through the use of the policy, objectives, audit results, analysis of data from performance assessment, corrective and preventive actions and management review. (4.6.1.1)

> The organization shall define and allocate the responsibility and authority for improvement of the management system. (4.6.1.2)

This is a restatement of the PDCA process of continual improvement that the policy, objectives, audit and data from the assessment processes are used to good effect and the management system is reviewed accordingly.

There are many tools available for implementing improvements to your IMS. Tools such as Baldridge, EFQM, British Quality Model (BQM), ISO 9004 and ISO 14031 all provide models that can be useful. Although some are specific to a particular discipline and some may be production/customer focused, the principles can often be extended generically. Such tools can be extremely helpful for internal benchmarking or comparisons between sites. They can also be effective scoring mechanisms for internal improvement. In such case care should be taken to ensure that the score becomes the end and not the means of improvement.

Corrective and preventive action

> A process shall be established to define requirements for:
>
> a) reviewing nonconformities or potential nonconformities (including interested parties' comments);
> b) determining the causes of nonconformities or potential nonconformities;
> c) evaluating the need for action to ensure that nonconformities do not occur or recur;
> d) determining and implementing the appropriate action needed;
> e) recording the results of action taken;
> f) reviewing the effectiveness of the action taken.
>
> Preventive and corrective actions shall be appropriate to the risks encountered. (4.6.2)

The level at which responsibility and authority for any specific action to deal with preventing nonconformance will obviously depend on the nature of the risk and the need to show commitment to the process at a senior level in the organization. There needs to be some process instigated to check that action has been taken and is effective in dealing with the root cause. As the model used for the IMS is proactive, the need for preventive action at this stage should be minimal and if not may indicate a failure in the aspect identification process.

We have already mentioned the need for processes for analysing and handling nonconformities. This phase of the management system seeks to establish a process for defining responsibility and authority for action. If a nonconformity has resulted in a dissatisfied customer, the immediate aim must be to take whatever actions are necessary to satisfy the customer as soon as possible. Then the root cause of the nonconformity should be eliminated to prevent a recurrence.

A measured response should be taken in dealing with nonconformities, so that it is appropriate to the effect of the failure (or the potential effect). The response should take account of the cost-effectiveness of the action, the likelihood of recurrence, and the consequences of not eliminating all prospects of related failures. The aim is to improve, and if the action is insufficient and does not eliminate the overall reason for failure, it will not meet this need.

Specific additional requirements of particular standards – improvement

In addition to the elements of PAS 99, provision needs to be made to meet the specific requirements of individual management system standards as follows.

ISO 9001:2000

8.5 Improvement (especially 8.5.3, preventive action).

ISO 14001:2004

No additional requirements.

BS OHSAS 18001:2007

No additional requirements.

Reference should always be made to the relevant standards to ensure that the specific requirements are met.

9. Management review

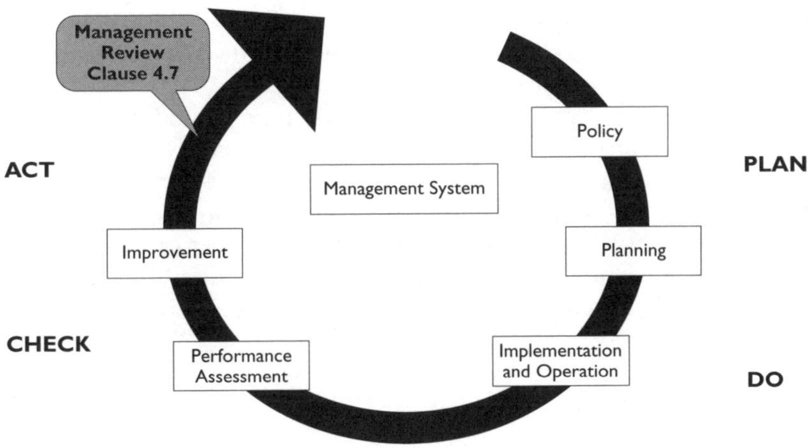

Figure 9.1

General

You may have used the ISR to establish where you are and where you want to be. The management review is in effect the same process, except you have a complete system in place. In this case the review is to establish whether your IMS fully meets your needs or if it should be extended or developed. You may for instance decide to extend the scope and carry out a gap analysis as per the ISR to fulfil the process of identifying actions needed.

> Top management shall review the organization's management system at planned intervals to ensure its continuing suitability, adequacy and effectiveness. (4.7.1.1)
>
> Reviews shall include assessing opportunities for improvement and the need for changes to the management system, including the policy and objectives. (4.7.1.2)
>
> Records of the management review shall be retained. (4.7.1.3)

The aim is to establish a process for reviewing the IMS at planned and regular intervals. This is one of the processes that will routinely attract attention from external assessors in the pursuit of establishing an organization's commitment to improvement.

Some may feel that fully fledged systems do not need improvement and 'if it ain't broke don't fix it'. In practice there are always regulatory, international and national moves to improve environmental and OH&S controls, so continual improvement is essential. Equally, in relation to quality, the expectations of the customer are unlikely to remain static. However, one of the main opportunities for improvement is in reviewing the system itself to ensure it is efficient as well as effective.

Input

> The input to management review shall include, as a minimum, information on:
>
> a) results of audits;
> b) interested party feedback;
> c) status of preventive and corrective actions;
> d) follow-up actions from previous management reviews;
> e) changing circumstances, including developments in legal and other requirements, related to the organization's aspects and associated risks;

f) recommendations for improvement;
g) data and information on the organization's performance;
h) results of the evaluation of compliance with legal and other requirements. (4.7.2)

The above is self-explanatory, but to help you in identifying feedback information, a checklist is provided below.

CHECKLIST

	Yes	No
Are management review meetings held regularly?	❑	❑
Has the frequency of the meetings been regularly considered and found appropriate?	❑	❑
Is each meeting held specifically for the purpose of management review, rather than as part of, say, a quarterly board meeting?	❑	❑
Is everyone involved who ought to be involved?	❑	❑
Are audit results available in advance of each meeting?	❑	❑
Are the reports submitted by, or on behalf of, each of the principal categories of stakeholder?	❑	❑
Are records kept of meetings and of decisions taken?	❑	❑
Are regular follow-up reports submitted on actions taken?	❑	❑
To what extent is the integrated system judged to be fulfilling its objectives?	❑	❑
What significant shortfalls have been identified?	❑	❑
What actions have been decided to correct the deficiencies?	❑	❑
Is the integrated management system judged to be adequate for the future of the organization?	❑	❑
What measures are to be taken to achieve continual improvement?	❑	❑

Output

> The output from the management review shall include any decisions and actions related to:
>
> a) improvement of the effectiveness of the management system;
> b) improvement related to interested party requirements;
> c) resource needs to enable improvement to the management system and its processes. (4.7.3)

The output should focus on the actions for improvement you have identified. It is implicit but needs to be restated that the policy itself and the objectives stemming from it may need to be revisited if the review process reveals shortcomings.

There can be problems in addressing stakeholder requirements and the solution may need to be finely balanced. In some cases the different groups will have conflicting requirements. A simple case would be where a new paint system is installed to improve product quality but the ensuing effluent causes environmental problems.

So there has to be some balancing and the IMS, if effective, should have addressed these conflicting requirements at the outset and made a more holistic response. If the review is responding to stakeholder pressure then the IMS should have a communication system in place that allows sensible interaction and discussion. At the end of the day, an organization that is trying to manage should not be so pilloried that it ceases operation.

Specific additional requirements of particular standards – management review

In addition to the elements of PAS 99, provision needs to be made to meet the specific requirements of individual management system standards as follows.

ISO 9001:2000

5.6 Management review (especially inputs having to include process performance and product conformity).

ISO 14001:2004

Complaints must be specifically included in the inputs to the review. (4.6)

BS OHSAS 18001:2007

Inputs to the management review must include complaints and the results of participation and consultation. (4.6)

Relevant outputs from the review must be made available for communication and consultation.

Reference should always be made to the relevant standards to ensure that the specific requirements are met.

Appendix 1. Elements of PAS 99 and references in this book

Requirements of PAS 99		**Page references in *IMS: Implementing and Operating***
4.1 General requirements		17
4.2 Management system policy		25
4.3 Planning		31
	4.3.1 Identification and evaluation of aspects, impacts and risks	32
	4.3.2 Identification of legal and other requirements	33
	4.3.3 Contingency planning	36
	4.3.4 Objectives	38
	4.3.5 Organizational structure, roles, responsibilities and authorities	41
4.4 Implementation and operation		49
	4.4.1 Operational control	51
	4.4.2 Management of resources	52
	4.4.3 Documentation requirements	55
	4.4.4 Communication	58
4.5 Performance assessment		61
	4.5.1 Monitoring and measurement	62
	4.5.2 Evaluation of compliance	67
	4.5.3 Internal audit	68
	4.5.4 Handling of nonconformities	70

4.6 Improvement		71
	4.6.1 General	71
	4.6.2 Corrective, preventive and improvement action	72
4.7 Management review		75
	4.7.1 General	75
	4.7.2 Input	76
	4.7.3 Output	78

Appendix 2. Common elements of quality, environmental and OH&S systems

Requirements of PAS 99	ISO 9001:2000	ISO 14001:2004	BS OHSAS 18001:2007
4.1 General requirements	4.1 5.5	4.1	4.1
4.2 Management system policy	5.1 5.3	4.2	4.2
4.3 Planning	5.4	4.3	4.3
4.3.1 Identification and evaluation of aspects, impacts and risks	5.2 5.4.2 7.2	4.3.1	4.3.1
4.3.2 Identification of legal and other requirements	5.3 7.2.1 7.2.2	4.3.2	4.3.2
4.3.3 Contingency planning	5.4 8.3	4.4.7	4.4.7
4.3.4 Objectives	5.4.1 5.4.2 8.5.1	4.3.3	4.3.3
4.3.5 Organizational structure, roles, responsibilities and authorities	5.1 5.5	4.4.1	4.4.1
4.4 Implementation and operation	7	4.4	4.4
4.4.1 Operational control	7	4.4.6	4.4.6
4.4.2 Management of resources	5.1 5.5.1 6	4.4.1 4.4.2	4.4.1 4.4.2
4.4.3 Documentation requirements	4.2	4.4.4 4.4.5 4.5.4	4.4.4 4.4.5 4.5.4

4.4.4 Communication	5.3 5.5.1 5.5.3 7.2.3	4.4.3	4.4.3
4.5 Performance assessment	8	4.5	4.5
4.5.1 Monitoring and measurement	8 7.6	4.5.1	4.5.1
4.5.2 Evaluation of compliance	8.2	4.5.2	4.5.1 4.5.2
4.5.3 Internal audit	8.2.2	4.5.5	4.5.5
4.5.4 Handling of nonconformities	8.3 8.4 8.5	4.5.3	4.5.3
4.6 Improvement	8.5	4.5.3 4.6	4.6
4.6.1 General	8.5	4.5.3 4.6	4.6
4.6.2 Corrective, preventive and improvement action	8.3 8.4 8.5	4.5.3	4.5.3
4.7 Management review	5.6	4.6	4.6
4.7.1 General	5.6.1	4.6	
4.7.2 Input	5.6.2	4.6	
4.7.3 Output	5.6.3	4.6	

Note: this table should be taken as a guide only, since correspondence between the clauses is often imprecise.

Appendix 3. An example of identification of processes in a manufacturing business

Scenario

The company is a manufacturing unit making consumer products. The raw materials it uses in its products are principally steel and plastics and the manufacturing processes are mainly machining, moulding, plating and painting.

The manufacturing processes have received close attention over the years with the main aims of product improvement and cost reduction. The cost reductions have come largely from increased mechanization, reducing the direct labour force, more efficient use of materials in reducing process scrap, refining designs by value engineering and a continual search for cheaper materials.

This has been allied to comprehensive quality and OH&S systems within the manufacturing shops, and addressing the significant environmental issues in the areas of atmospheric discharges (paint shop) and effluent (principally from plating). Outside the immediate manufacturing area, however, these subjects received less attention.

The factory is an old building on a site that is fenced, bordering on to other business units and close to domestic properties. The company has owned the site for 125 years.

At the macro scale, its operations are outlined in Figure A3.1. However, the operations include many processes in the 'life-cycle', from raw materials, extraction, etc. to final disposal, as shown in Figure A3.2; there are many sub-processes as well. The processing on site is fairly well mapped because of the existing ISO 9001 and ISO 14001 arrangements.

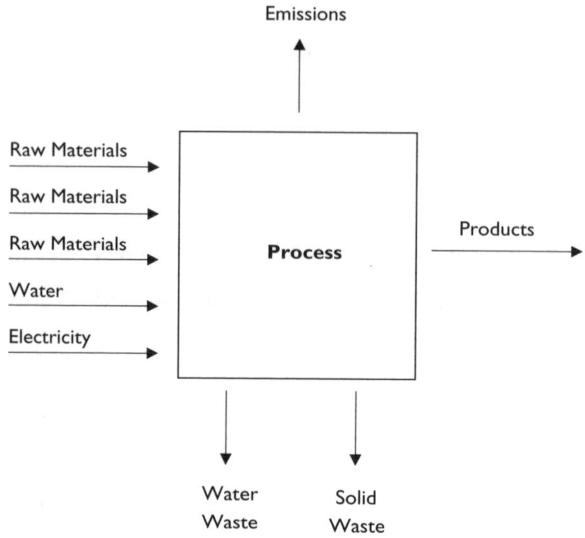

Figure A3.1

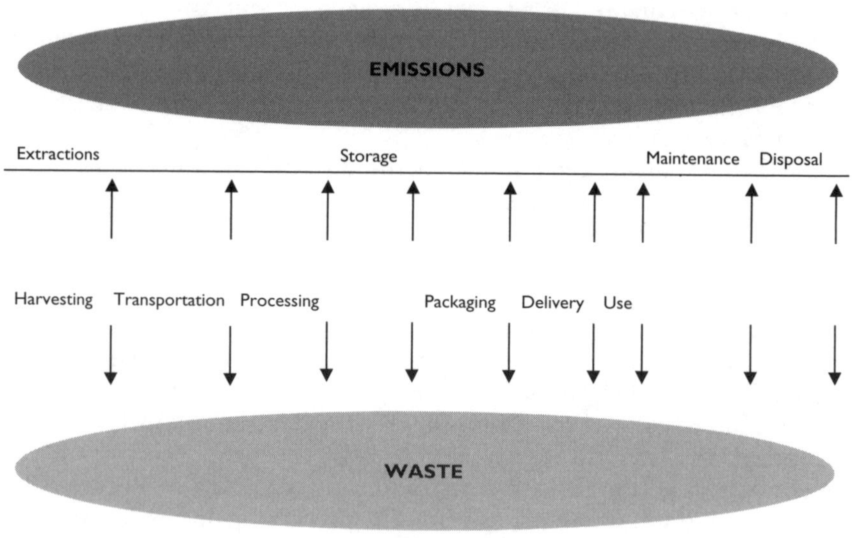

Figure A3.2

Extraction and harvesting

Most of the raw materials are purchased from suppliers based in the UK, but some of the materials used originate from Eastern Europe, the timber for packaging is harvested from a Scandinavian forest, and the paints come mainly from secondary producers. The company has no direct control over the processes involved but there are indirect aspects that could impact on the quality and environment. There is perhaps no OH&S aspect they can reasonably be expected to control on a day-to-day basis. It can, however, reasonably be expected to specify the safety standards it would wish to be applied and assess suppliers to establish that those specified are being met or exceeded. The company's environmental management system (EMS) had failed to address this issue, which should be included in its aspect register.

Transport to site

This is a process partially beyond its control, but is an indirect aspect in the environmental element of the system. In this case it does not have the potential to affect the quality. The way the truck drivers manoeuvre at the site means this process needs to be considered from an OH&S viewpoint.

Integration of the EMS and OH&S management systems into the quality management system (QMS) would have failed because this was not in the company's QMS scope.

Storage

These activities have direct aspects and the storage process may need to be broken down into sub-processes for evaluation, as shown in Figure A3.3. (This is a simple example. The reality may often be more complex – for example if hazardous substances are involved.)

Only part of this process was covered by the QMS, the rest was part of the EMS and OH&S systems.

Processing

This area is well mapped and understood and could be presented in a fashion such as shown in Figure 3.6 on page 23.

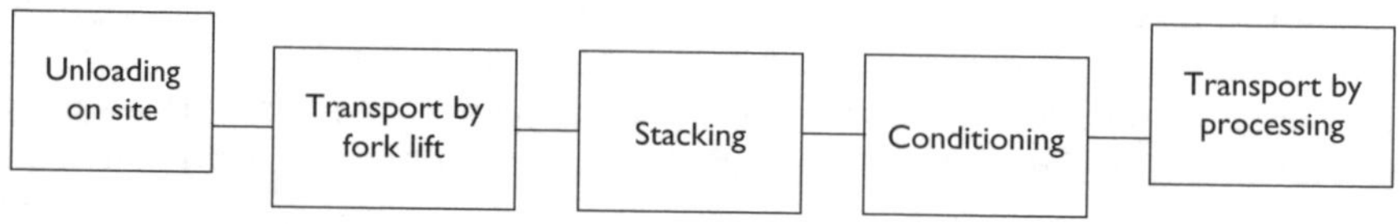

Figure A3.3

Following the first identification of aspects and their prioritization and control measures, it will be seen whether these activities need to be closely considered or can be discounted. The OH&S, environmental and quality aspects have been understood for some time and effective control measures were in operation.

Packaging

As illustrated in Figure 3.6 on page 23, there are many stages involved that needed to be considered in the evaluation exercise.

Because it was not seen as part of the manufacturing operation this activity had not received the same attention as the production operations and the costs and environmental aspects had been largely ignored. The controls on packaging waste in Europe are strictly applied, and issues such as manual handling and quality are equally important.

Delivery

Here, the organization has far more control of this operation to its customer than it has over the raw materials being delivered to it, so direct aspects arise, such as:

- selection of transportation;
- manner in which transportation services are operated;
- driving of vehicles;
- loading of vehicles;
- unloading of vehicles;
- working conditions;
- driver training.

As this had not formed part of the manufacturing process it was not part of the current quality system apart from ensuring customer satisfaction with the delivery arrangements. It had similarly received minimal attention from OH&S and environmental viewpoints in spite of occasional complaints about noise from nearby residents. There is a need to remember the OH&S requirements with regard to such matters as mechanical handling and the drivers' hours of duties.

Use

This cannot normally have direct aspects if the organization has behaved ethically, at the strategic level, in determining its product range. (An organization making fertilizer cannot necessarily be held responsible if a terrorist organization finds that it can be used as a raw material for explosive devices.) However, the company needed to consider the processes in normal use to determine whether there are aspects that could have a significant impact. It cannot control all the OH&S arrangements in use, but it should identify any hazards associated with the goods in normal use.

This is of growing importance in view of increasingly stringent consumer protection legislation.

Maintenance

As with 'Use', this needs to be considered at the sub-process level to establish if there are significant aspects. This has indirect aspects with respect to environment and quality but probably not with the OH&S element of the IMS.

Ultimate disposal of product

As with 'Use' and 'Maintenance', there may be a number of processes which the company can indirectly influence, but they will probably have only environmental aspects. Increasingly disposal instructions form part of the user instructions with consumer products (batteries, aerosols, paint, etc.).

Caution

This is a very simplistic example and in reality the Processing Stage will probably be much more complex. Consideration needs to be given to all non-core activities on site, such as:

- office work;
- contractors;
- cleaning activities;
- maintenance;
- repair;
- normal, abnormal, emergency situations;
- use of buildings, resources.

The EMS also needed to review past activities on site in order to establish if past practices had led to any land or water pollution. Such information was not available as such from the Quality System but the site plans and OH&S records of employee health problems enabled the company to identify some areas of concern.

Conclusion

It is only when quality, environment and OH&S are seen as part of an IMS covering the total activities of the company – not just those directly concerned with production – that the importance of the ancillary aspects becomes apparent.

Appendix 4. Marshalls plc

This appendix shows examples of documents used by Marshalls plc (who have kindly consented to their publication) in the implementation of an IMS in one of their quarries, within their Natural Stone Division, producing paving slabs, aggregate, etc.

They are included not as a pattern but purely to illustrate the way in which one organization planned its objectives as it progresses towards the implementation of an IMS. Flow diagrams of the processes used to win the stone, cutting, etc. are included to show the processes the organization is evaluating to determine aspects.

Marshalls

Integrated Management System Appleton Quarry

Integrated Management System – Programme of Objectives – update

Aspect	Benefit	Input	Target Date	Output	Target Date	Process Owner	Resource requirement	Monitoring method
IMS Awareness 1	Reduced risk by improved awareness	Highlight potential risks & hazards	Oct 2001	Provide appropriate 'signage' throughout the site for less than £1000	Nov 2001	DS DB DC	3 Man days + external resource + £	Photographic evidence before & after
IMS Awareness 2	Legal & Regulatory Requirement	Develop site plan	Nov 2001	Provide information for all stakeholders and regulatory bodies	Nov 2001	DS Mac KP	Man days	Production of Documented site plan
IMS Awareness 3	Increased awareness reducing potential for accidents and environmental incidents	Highlight risk and Hazards To all stakeholders	Nov 2001	To produce guidance document for subcontractors & tenants and communicate	Dec 2001	IMS Steering team	Man days	Documented process, evidence of acknowledgement
IMS Training	Raised awareness – provide information for future development	Promote IMS strategy to stakeholders	Sept 2001	Develop & communicate information package to stakeholders	Dec 2001	IMS Steering Team	Time	Documentary evidence – training records
Legal & other requirements	Demonstrate compliance with legislation & other requirements	Identify all legal and regulatory requirements H&S, Env & Q	Dec 2001	Ensure compliance with corporate policy	Feb 2001	Group QMS ENV H & S	Time	Internal assessment of requirements
Site pedestrian access	Improved safety	Review current access & improve	Aug 2001	To provide safe access for visitors from car park to office	Nov 2001	DS	Human & financial	Before & After photograph
Emergency plan & Response	Legal & regulatory Compliance	Develop H & S and Environment emergency plan	Draft Oct 2001	Implement, communicate & practise	Dec 2001	DC DS DB CR	Human & Time	Process Plan Records of implementation Training records

Colour Code Key **Project on target** **Project Completed** **Project Behind Schedule**

Appendix 4

Overview

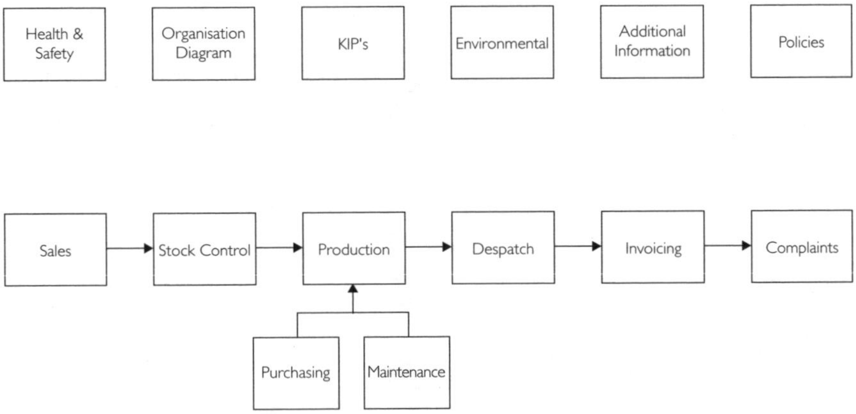

Appleton Quarry Process Flow Map

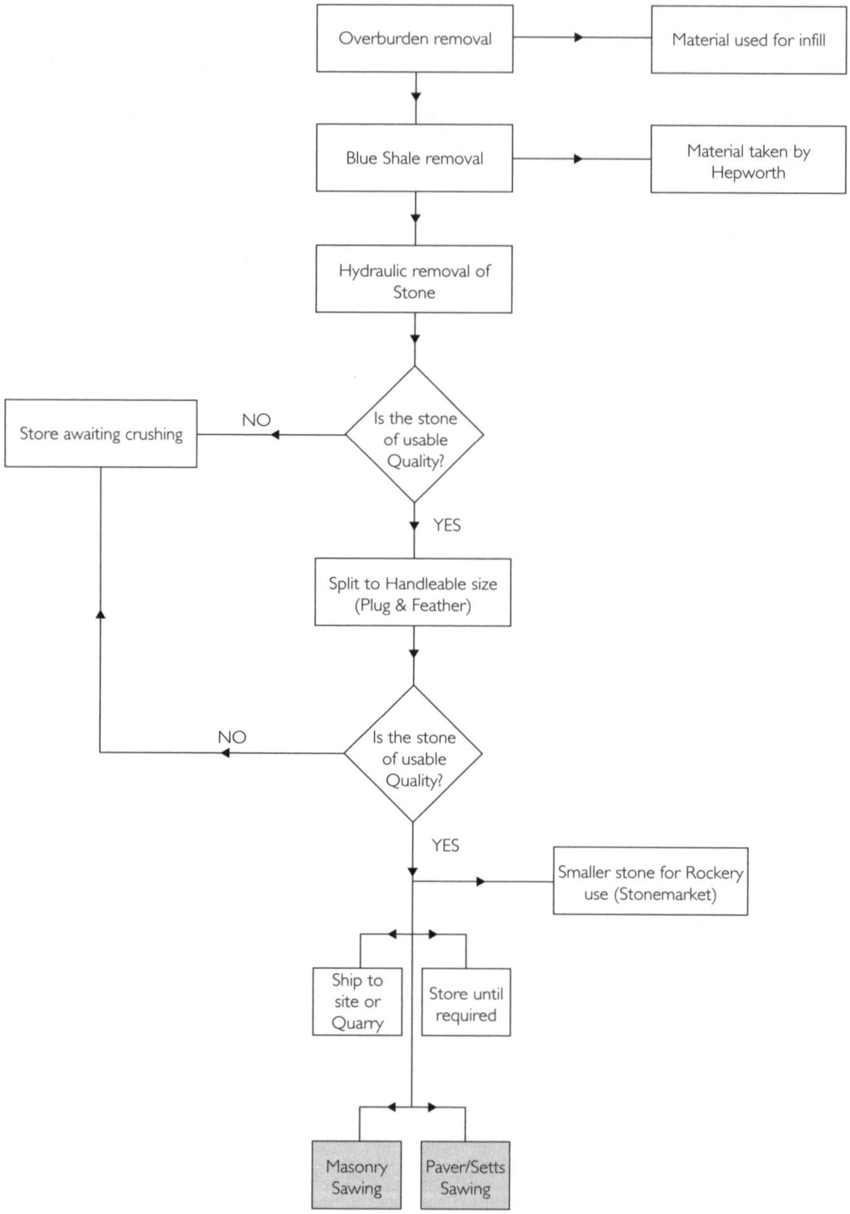

Appleton Paver/Setts Saw

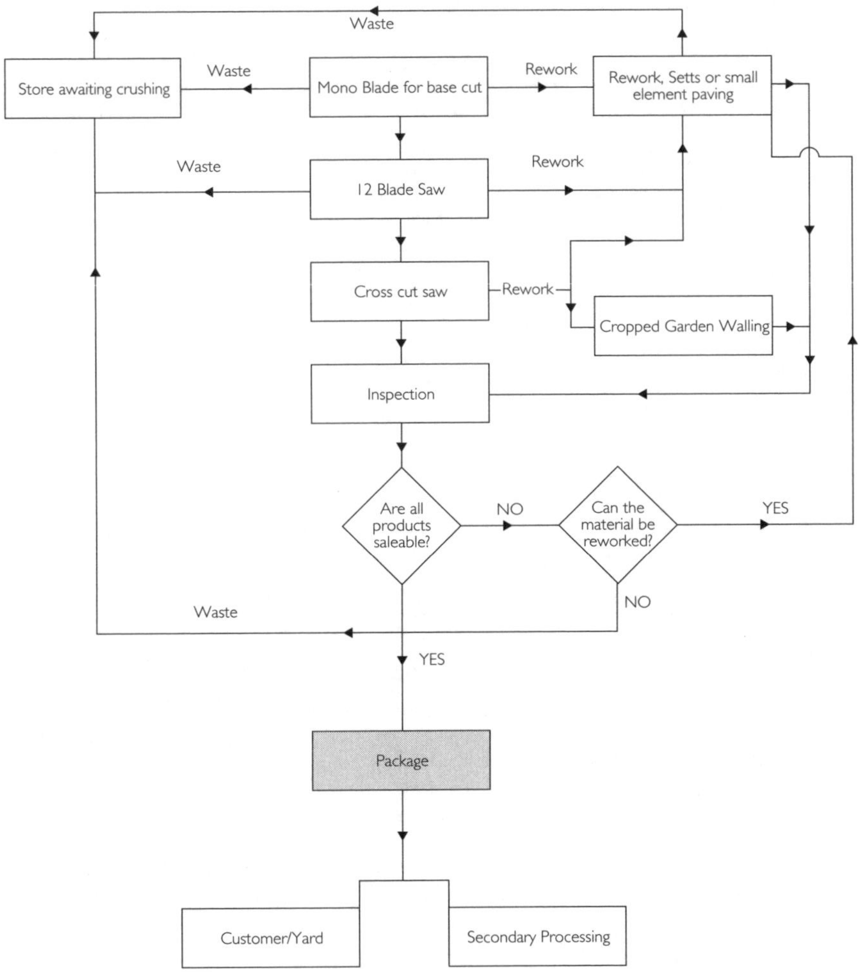

Appleton Masonry Saw

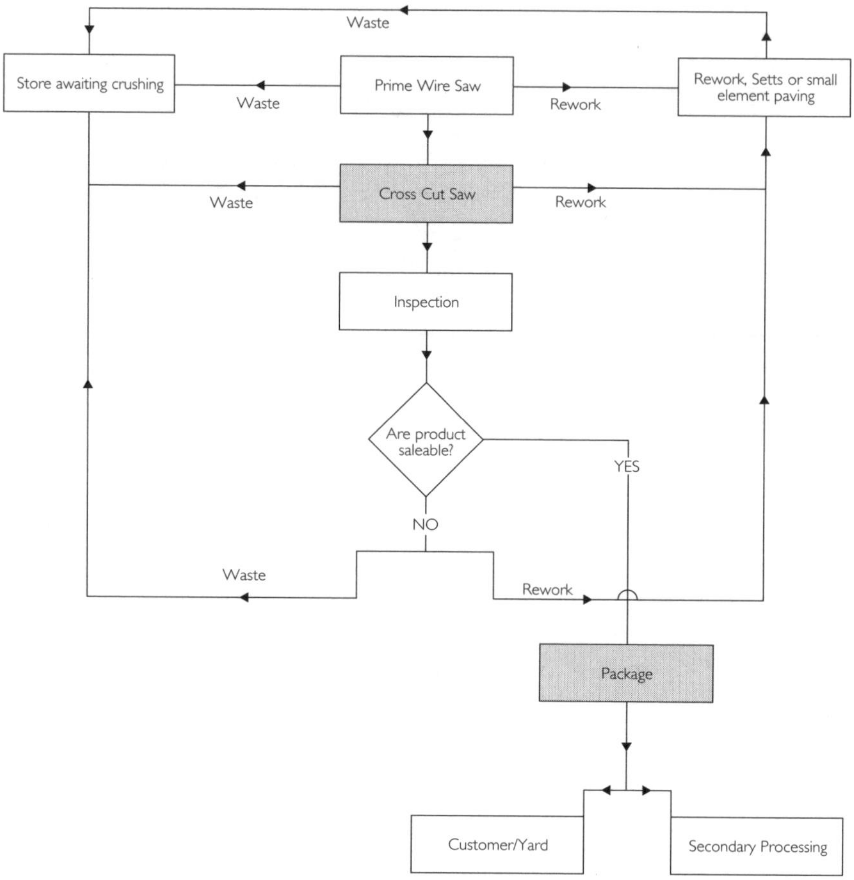

Appendix 5. AMEC Capital Projects Ltd

AMEC has developed an IMS in its AMEC Capital Projects Construction Division, which has been registered by BSI Global Quality Services with respect to ISO 9001, ISO 14001 and OHSAS 18001.

AMEC has kindly granted permission for the inclusion of some of its documentation to illustrate its approach with regards to its system, policy, responsibilities, etc.

THE INTEGRATED MANAGEMENT OF SAFETY, HEALTH, ENVIRONMENT & QUALITY

CONTENTS

THE INTEGRATED MANAGEMENT OF SAFETY, HEALTH, ENVIRONMENT & QUALITY

1 Introduction

AMEC Capital Projects Construction Division (ACPL-CD) has adopted an Integrated Management System (IMS) for the management of Safety, Health, Environment and Quality along with other key disciplines within project management.

The integration covers all aspects of a project including design, procurement, management, construction, and engineering processes. The interfaces between these elements are identified within a Project Management Plan (PMP).

The PMP effectively combines the requirements of ISO 9001, ISO 14001 and OHSAS 18001, AMEC standards, stakeholder requirements, company procedures and the associated legislation for Safety, Health and the Environment (See Figure 1).

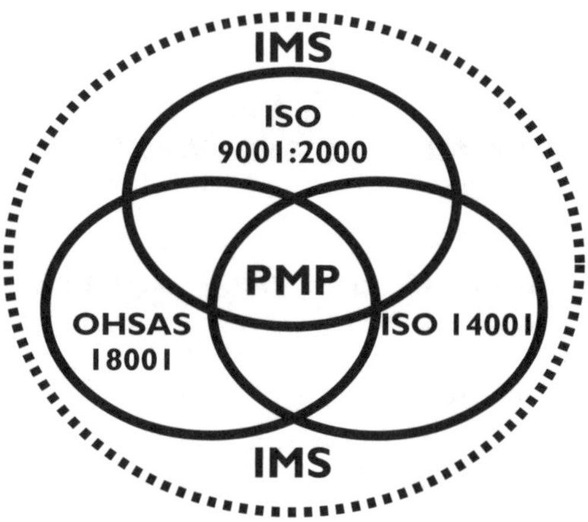

Figure 1 – PMP Development

1.1 IMS Background and System Development

Experience shows that in operating successful systems for Quality, Safety, Health and Environmental, in respect of managing a business or project, they are inextricably linked and in many cases overlap.

The need to define objectives, policy, organisation, management responsibilities, procedures and performance indicators are common to all and often duplicated in each. In order to simplify the management arrangements whilst maintaining clearly defined requirements and adequate resources for each management discipline, ACPL-CD believe that the use of one comprehensive Integrated Management System provides benefits to all parties involved.

2 Integrated Management System Overview

The overview in Figure 2 demonstrates the document framework that spans from the Division to projects with regard to Safety, Health & Environmental and Quality.

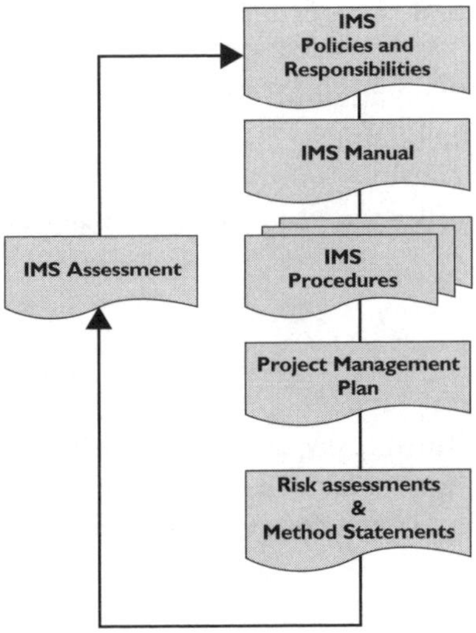

Figure 2

2.1 Policies

The policies that form the basis of the IMS, are the Quality, Safety, Health and Environmental Policies, which are signed by the Director with S, H&E and Quality responsibilities.

The specific Safety, Health and Environmental Policy Statement of Intent – see Figure 3 – incorporating specific safety, health and environment objectives also includes the management responsibilities for implementation of the policy and the arrangements therein.

The policies demonstrate commitment and establish an overall sense of direction and principles for action.

2.2 Organisation & Responsibilities

Specific S, H&E responsibilities for employees (See Figure 4) are included within the policy documentation to ensure that a clear understanding of individuals responsibilities is communicated.

The IMS is supported by a team of professional managers and advisers. This support is provided by either the core team and/or full time site based personnel.

The main objectives of the Core IMS team as a support service are to:

- Co-ordinate the development of appropriate processes and procedures for the business
- Assist in project establishment
- Facilitate the monitoring of performance against the established systems.

2.3 IMS Manual

The Company IMS Manual provides a holistic perspective on how the integrated management system fits together, works, manages interface and the IMS compliance with the relevant standards.

2.4 Implementation and Operation

S, H&E performance is synonymous with quality. Since we are committed to excellence we continue to define our objectives and develop techniques of implementation for achieving continuous improvement in accident reduction. This is further achieved through competent supervision, training, information and communication.

AMEC Capital Projects Limited
Safety, Health and Environment Policy
General Statement of Intent

amec

1. AMEC Capital Projects Limited considers successful safety, health and environmental management to be of prime importance to its business and is committed to continual improvement in safety, health and environmental standards.
2. It is the policy of AMEC Capital Projects Limited to:
   - Pursue high standards of safety, health and environmental management as an integral part of efficient management of the business and ensure that decisions about other priorities take proper account of safety, health and environmental requirements;
   - Comply with all legislative requirements and the AMEC group policy pertaining to safety, health and the environment as the minimum standard;
   - Develop systems and procedures that deliver the high standards sought, and in particular provide for:
     - Well maintained plant and systems of work that are safe and without risk to health or the environment;
     - Suitable arrangements for the selection, use, handling, storage and transport of articles and substances;
     - Adequate information, instruction, training and supervision to enable work to be carried out safely and without risk to the environment by persons with the necessary competence;
     - Safe premises and work places, including access to and egress from them;
     - Safe and healthy working environments with adequate welfare facilities;
     - Designs which recognise, include and apply safe practice during preparation, construction and subsequent operational use and maintenance after completion of the project, and which consider environmental impact;
     - Prevention of polluting emissions to air, land or water;
     - Management of the use of natural resources;
     - Control of noise, dust, smell, vibration, traffic movement or other nuisance or environmental effects which may cause offence to the local community or environment;
     - Waste minimisation;
     - Management of waste disposal including recycling where appropriate;
     - Communications, health surveillance and advisory facilities as required.
   - Develop and review clear safety, health and environmental performance indicators including:
     - accident and incident performance;
     - annual safety, health and environmental objectives;
     - training achievement;
     - audits.
   - Review and, if necessary, revise this policy on an annual basis.

3 The managing directors have overall responsibility for this policy. AMEC Capital Projects Limited has appointed a director in each division to be responsible for safety, health and environment whose responsibilities are set out in the policy documents.

4 AMEC Capital Projects Limited will produce and update detailed organisation and arrangements, and all necessary resources will be made available, for the implementation of this policy.

5 It is the responsibility of management and employees to implement this policy together with their collective and individual responsibilities. Individuals' responsibilities under this policy are set out in the policy documents.

6 AMEC Capital Projects Limited will appoint competent safety, health and environmental managers/advisers whose duties are set out in the policy documents.

Signed David Robson
David Robson
Managing Director
Mechanical and Electrical Division
AMEC Capital Projects Limited
Date: 6 April 2001

Signed
A B Lamerton
Managing Director
Construction Division
AMEC Capital Projects Limited
Date: 6 April 2001

Figure 3 – S, H&E Policy

			Relevant individual responsibilities in health and safety policy																			
			a	b	c	d	e	f	g	h	i	j	k	l	m	n	o	p	q	r	s	t
Title Holder		**Page ref**																				
Managing Director	Directors	11	•	•	•	•	•	•	•	•												
Director with safety responsibility		12	•	•	•	•	•	•	•	•	•	•	•	•	•							
Directors of Operations		15	•	•	•	•	•	•	•	•	•	•	•	•								
All other directors		16	•	•	•	•	•	•	•													
Senior person in control of work location (manager) not specified elsewhere	Managers	17/18	•	•	•	•	•	•	•	•	•	•	•	•	•	•	•	•	•	•	•	
Departmental heads / managers		19	•	•	•	•	•	•	•	•	•	•										
Administration manager		19	•	•	•	•	•	•		•	•	•										
Human Resource managers		20	•	•	•	•	•															
Labour managers/industrial relation manager		21	•																			
Area / Regional Construction / Project /Contracts managers		17/18	•	•	•	•	•	•	•	•	•	•	•	•	•	•	•	•	•	•	•	
Contract Administrator		17/18	•	•	•			•														
Site Managers		17/18	•	•	•	•	•	•	•	•	•	•	•	•	•	•	•	•	•	•	•	
Site / Section Agents		17/18	•	•	•	•	•	•	•	•	•	•	•	•	•	•	•	•	•	•	•	
All Construction / Services / Eng / M&E / Electrical Managers		17/18	•	•	•	•	•	•	•	•	•	•	•	•	•	•	•	•	•	•	•	
Office Managers (incl. site based)		17/18	•	•	•	•	•	•	•	•	•	•	•	•			•	•	•	•	•	
Chief engineer**		17/18	•	•	•	•	•	•	•	•	•	•	•	•	•	•	•	•	•	•	•	
**Additionally for these engineers		23	•	•	•	•	•	•	•													
All Engineers/Planners/ Estimators	Specialists	23	•	•	•	•	•	•	•													
Project leader		23	•	•	•	•	•	•	•													
Project co-ordinator		23	•	•	•	•	•	•	•													
Procurement personnel/buyers		22	•	•	•	•	•	•	•	•	•											
Storeman (works and site)		26	•	•	•	•	•	•	•	•	•	•										
Plant inspector/operator trainer		26	•		•	•	•	•				•										
Plant inspector/operator trainer		24/25		•			•				•			•		•						
SHE Controllers		13/14	•	•	•	•	•	•	•	•	•	•	•	•	•	•	•	•	•	•	•	•
Safety manager/advisers		24/25	•	•	•	•	•	•	•	•	•	•	•	•	•	•	•	•				
Safety co-ordinator		24	•	•				•	•	•	•	•	•	•		•						
Architects / Designers		23	•	•	•	•	•	•	•													
All Construction / Services / Eng M&E / Electrical Supervisors	Supervisors	27/28	•	•	•	•	•	•	•	•	•	•	•	•	•	•	•	•	•	•	•	
General foreman		27/28	•	•	•	•	•	•	•	•	•	•	•	•	•	•	•	•	•	•	•	
Trades / joinery foreman / supervisors		27/28	•	•	•	•	•	•	•	•	•	•	•	•	•	•	•	•	•	•	•	
Gangers		27/28	•	•	•	•		•	•	•	•	•	•	•	•	•	•	•	•	•	•	
Chargehands		27/28	•	•	•	•		•	•	•	•	•	•	•	•	•	•	•	•	•	•	
All employees in addition to the above		29	•	•	•	•	•	•	•	•	•	•	•	•	•	•						

Note: Senior, Assistant, Sub, Deputy, section etc. have the same duties as the main title holder.

Figure 4 – Responsibility Matrix

2.5 Procedures

In order to promote uniformity of working methods, irrespective of the project or contract organisation, certain fundamental procedures are operated across the business, without significant deviation. The Project Management Plan identifies the specific procedures that are required for a particular location/project. This allows for the tailoring of the system to the end users needs.

Common IMS mechanisms have been identified within the procedures in areas such as risk assessment, induction, training and monitoring arrangements.

Evolution of the IMS has also seen Process and Activity Maps, developed from the written procedure, as a means of transferring knowledge to the recipient in a user friendly manner.

2.6 The Integrated Project Management Plan

One of the main operating features of the IMS is the Project Management Plan, the compilation of which is shown diagrammatically in Figure 1. It is this document that combines the requirements of ISO 9001, ISO 14001 and OHSAS 18001 and is the main link between the business systems and projects.

The plan is designed to embrace all work undertaken by the Company, consultants, contractors and suppliers. The plan is developed on a modular basis to allow project specific requirements to be addressed.

The purpose of the plan is to define the system for managing S, H&E and Quality on the project and to identify the requirements of the interfaces with processes such as design, procurement, processes etc.

2.7 Risk Management

Hazard Identification and Risk Assessment underpins work activity and is generated not only by the team responsible for the activity but also benefits from input by Safety, Health, Environmental and Quality professionals.

To ensure the transparency of the process there are various mechanisms within the management system which allows for effective feedback into the hazard identification and risk assessment process.

2.8 Environmental Code of Practice

Within the Project Management Plan the core environmental management procedures are identified in the ACPL-CD Environmental Code of Practice ECoP (See Figure 5) for construction, including operations and maintenance activities.

The principal aim of the ECoP is to provide an effective environmental management tool based on the requirements of ISO. The ECoP supplies a robust framework for environmental management, which due to its flexible nature can be expanded to include any additional requirements. In this way, the company environmental (S, H&E) policy, legislative requirements and specific contract requirements are effectively implemented on site and a framework for monitoring environmental performance is provided.

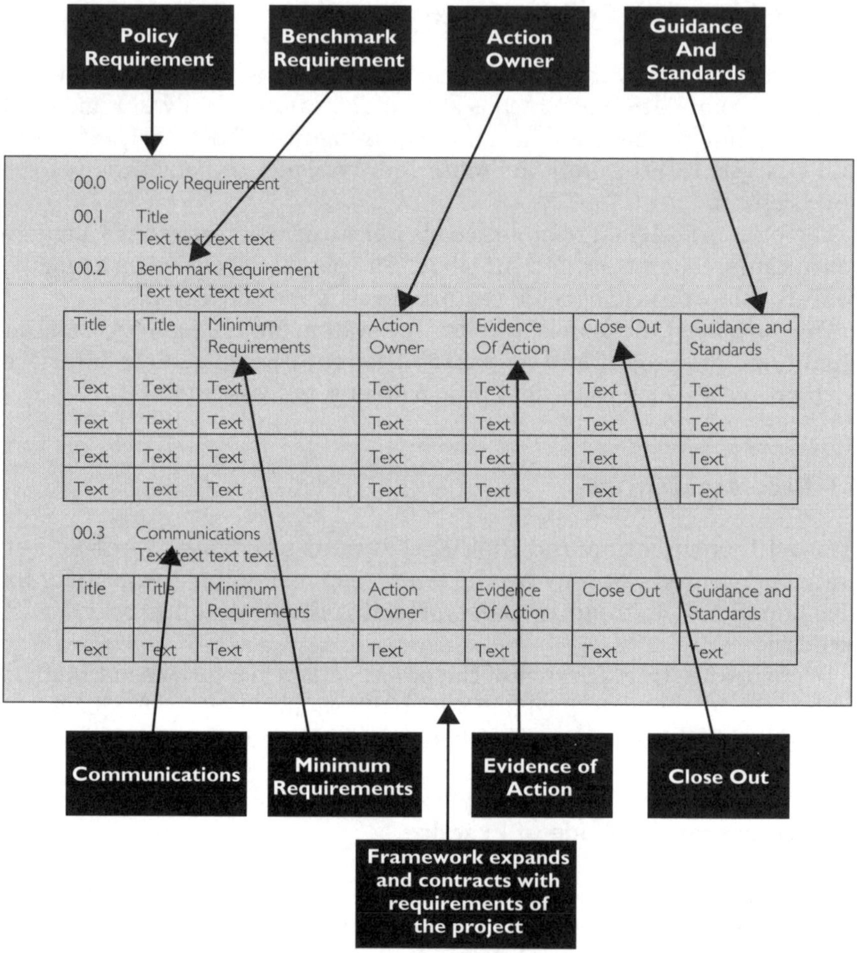

Figure 5 – ECoP

2.9 Communication

When the management system has been established for a process or project, the primary requirement is to then ensure that the system is deployed into safe conditions and safe behaviours. These requirements are achieved by the following:

- Ongoing monitoring and review of the policy and management system to ensure they remain 'live' and appropriate to the business needs.
- Involvement of all relevant parties in the process of risk assessment and safe systems of work to ensure the assessments and systems are suitable and sufficient and at the correct standard for the work being carried out.
- Defined responsibilities for key personnel.
- A structured induction programme for all new starters, contractors and third parties such as visitors.
- Provision of an IMS information system such as the intranet (see Figure 6) project bulletins, briefings, posters, alerts and updates. This may include information on near miss incidents, legislation updates, best practice initiatives, etc.
- Structured IMS monitoring that includes inspections, tours, meetings, response systems.
- A comprehensive audit and assessment programme by both internal and external bodies.
- Use of supervisor's S, H&E checklists.
- The adoption of the Views of Operatives In the Construction Environment (VOICE) scheme, based on a behavioural approach to IMS related matters.
- Training for management, operatives, staff and VOICE observers.
- IMS core briefs for personnel.
- The measurement and reporting of performance results.
- Initiatives for making contributions to any health, safety, environmental and quality matters including systems of work, design etc.

2.10 Measurement

ACPL-CD are piloting an IMS assessment process. The process is based on the assessment of performance as opposed to traditional compliance auditing and is a key driver for continual improvement.

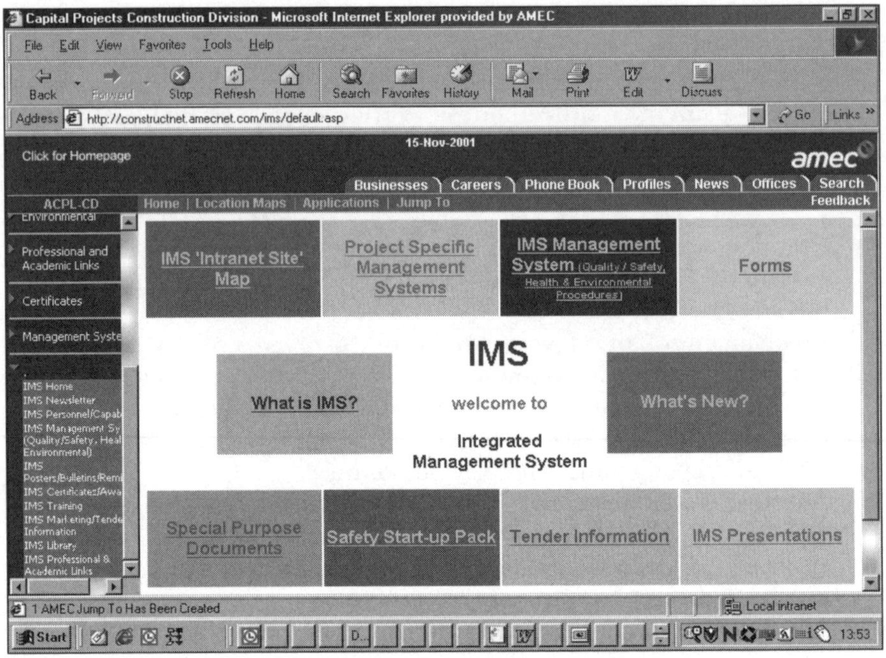

Figure 6 – IMS Intranet Front Page

2.11 Feedback and Consultation

The establishment of Improvement Groups and involvement of end users ensures that procedures, initiatives and arrangements are continuously reviewed in terms of their value to the business. The feedback and information is cascaded through the organisation to achieve a positive climate, as distinct from merely increasing awareness to health, safety, quality, welfare and environmental issues.

This system of feedback will be demonstrated in meetings, briefings, reports etc, which communicate key issues for the period to all the management staff and employees through formal communication lines.

Bibliography

Standards and specifications

BS 6079-1:2002, *Project management – Part 1: Guide to project management*
BS 8800:2004, *Occupational health and safety management systems – Guide*
BS 8900:2006, *Guidance for managing sustainable development*
BS 31100, *Code of practice for risk management* (yet to be published)
BS EN ISO 22000:2005, *Food safety management systems – Requirements for any organization in the food chain*
BS ISO/IEC 20000-1:2005, *Information technology – Service management – Part 1: Specification*
BS ISO/IEC 27001:2005, BS 7799-2:2005, *Information technology – Security techniques – Information security management systems – Requirements*
BS OHSAS 18001:2007, *Occupational health and safety management systems – Requirements*
ISO 9000:2005, *Quality management systems – Fundamentals and vocabulary*
ISO 9001:2000, *Quality management systems – Requirements*
ISO 9004:2000, *Quality management systems – Guidelines for performance improvements*
ISO 14001:2004, *Environmental management systems – Requirements with guidance for use*
ISO 14004:2004, *Environmental management systems – General guidelines on principles, systems and support techniques*
ISO 14031:2000, *Environmental management – Environmental performance evaluation – Guidelines*
ISO Guide 72:2001, *Guidelines for the justification and development of management system standards*
ISO/IEC Guide 73:2002, *Risk management – Vocabulary – Guidelines for use in standards*
PAS 99:2006, *Specification of common management system requirements as a framework for integration*

Other publications

Hinch, H (2003) *IMS: Managing Food Safety,* BSI, London
IMS Risk Solutions (2003) *IMS: Creating a Manual,* BSI, London
Karapetrovic et al. (2006) *Dynamics and integration of standardized management systems,* Documentaria Universitaria, Universitat de Girona, Girona
MacGregor Associates (1997) *Management System Standards* (HB 10138), BSI, London
Murray, P (2003) *IMS: Information Security,* BSI, London
Smith, D and Politowski, R (2007) *IMS: A Framework for Integrated Management Systems – Background to PAS 99 and its application* (BIP 2119), BSI, London
Smith, D and Green, C (2005) *Managing the Environment the ISO 14001 Way* (BIP 2069), BSI, London